MANUFACTURED BY THE VIEL-O-PHONE CO. LTD. BOMBAY
TRADE MARK
VIEL-O-PHONE
1074
Mr. Goswami
VR 1567

The
TAJ RECORD
EMBLEM OF PERFECTION
HINDI SONG
HRT. 89 K
मोहन मुर्ली वाले तुम पर लाखों परनाम
भजन
Master GOPAL KRISHNA

The TWIN
TWIN
HINDUSTANI SONG
FT.3365
Miss DURGA
OPH. 387
MANUFACTURED FOR THE TWIN RECORD CO. LTD. DUM DUM

GRAMOPHONE CONCERT RECORD
MADE IN GERMANY
TRADE MARK
PATENTED PATENTED
Manufactured by
The Gramophone Company, Limited,
and Sister Companies.
HINDUSTANI FEMALE SONG
BHAIRVI-TITALA
sung by Janki Bai
ALLAHABAD
G. C.-3-13645

MADE IN INDIA
YOUNG INDIA
MESSAGE
TM 8307
THE NATIONAL GRAMOPHONE RECORD MANUFACTURING CO. LTD. BOMBAY

JALSA

WOMEN AND THEIR JOURNEYS FROM THE SALON TO THE STUDIO

Vidya Shah

Published for
External Publicity & Public Diplomacy Division
Ministry of External Affairs, Government of India

Published by
Tulika Books
in association with
Centre for Media and Alternative Communication

First edition 2016

ISBN: 978-93-82381-77-8

Design: **Parthiv Shah**
Design assistance: **Anita Channer, Neha Passi**

Research assistance: **Hemal Shringla, Kshitij Katiyar, Naresh Kumar**
Copyediting and coordination: **Kshitij Katiyar**
Copy assistance: **Kaveri Acharya, Ananyaa Gaur**
Photo editor: **Parthiv Shah**

Printed at: **Lustra Print Process Pvt. Ltd.**

Contents

Acknowledgments

This effort has been made possible with inputs and assistance from various people who have contributed to the project immensely. We are particularly grateful to:

Amlan Das Gupta

Amrit Gangar

Anil Relia

Anjan Chakraverty

Ashish Bhadra

Deepti Priya Mehrotra

Jyotindra Jain

Krishna Kant Rastogi

Lakshmi Vishwanathan

Pandit Birju Maharaj

Pramod K.G.

Rajeev Patke

Rajendra Prasad

Saleem Kidwai

Sharmila Tagore

Shyam Benegal

Sidharth Bhatia

Suresh Chandvankar

S. Kalidas

Vibodh Parthasarathi

Vidushi Girija Devi

V. Sriram

Preface

The idea of "Women on Record" came to me a few years ago when I was introduced to early recorded music by a music lover in the audience after one of my performances. The music that was given to me on cassettes was quite unclear, garbled and scratchy as these were old gramophone recordings. I could certainly identify some traditional compositions which are typically taught and found in notated collections of compositions. There was also devotional music and lighter popular songs that are very much a part of public memory. I realized that while there were names to these voices, some very well known at that, there wasn't too much that one could readily find out about them. They were the women on the record, of whom there was little record.

Over the last five years, the Centre for Media and Alternative Communication (CMAC) has become a veritable archive with music, visuals, stories, film and other such documentation. Through extensive travels across the world and meetings with collectors, music connoisseurs and academics this indeed has been a rich experience in re-documenting what was on record. Apart from meeting with relevant people in India, extensive conversations with organizations like Excavated Shellac (California), the British Library in London and the Max Planck Institute in Berlin have made the journey much richer. Images of the performance spaces by Parthiv Shah bring alive the resplendent period.

With its arrival in early 20th century India, the gramophone democratized the musical space. The machine made possible a much easier interaction between the listener and the artiste than was possible earlier. This subsequently, in many ways, has given contemporary artistes privileges that were perhaps unthinkable for artistes in those days. For instance, I get on to the stage and perform what I have received from my Gurus with gratitude; I sing to all kinds of audiences from very diverse backgrounds and, importantly, I have the freedom to choose my repertoire. But the truth is that some of this music comes with considerable social baggage, as it is the music of robust, entertaining courtesans. I even wonder if they had the privilege to enjoy it as much as I can afford to; if pleasure was an agency they felt they had a right to!

As the vinyl makes a comeback to the world of recorded music in the 21st century, it seems to me to be a poignant time to go back into a historical journey to understand the milieu in which it all began. *Jalsa* takes you through this journey from the salon to the studio. It is an effort to give an insight, a perspective, on the beginning of the interface of technology and entertainment, and the irreversible impact it has had on how we listen to, enjoy and consume music; an acknowledgement of an important slice of the history of Indian music which is celebrated the world over today in its many forms and avatars.

From the Salon to the Studio

Music has been a very central aspect of Indian culture – there is a song for every occasion. Through spiritual beginnings and underpinnings to intellectual moorings and even entertainment, the many worlds of Indian music are an integral part of our social fabric. And to think that this is largely an oral tradition that has been handed down through generations of singers and performers makes it seem even more fantastic in its resilience and its ability to survive. From simple chants to more sophisticated systems and stylistic genres – classical, devotional, popular and film – this music has evolved considerably through centuries. And various 20th-century artistes have played an important role in putting it on the world map and today it is in a place where it is recognized, enjoyed and even practised (non-Indians included) across the world.

This also happens at a time when it is hard to think of a world where one cannot access music to one's liking as and when one wants it. Music is now really a part of the larger idea of how we consume entertainment. With the onslaught of various kinds of technology that have made this access possible, there has also been a blurring of boundaries, a slew of crossovers and generally a panacea of possibilities. Sufi-rock, electronica, dub-funk, EDM, ethnic electronica and many more; this noveau list only adding to the already existing grand dames like Classical, Spiritual (Qawwali or Gospel, for instance), Jazz, Rock and Reggae. A lot of this has been made possible largely with the introduction of technology into the production of sound.

It all began a little over a hundred years ago when Indian music was first captured on technology. This changed the listening experience of music, perhaps forever. It opened a new chapter and paved the way for the making of singing sensations, stars and redefined the world of entertainment in ways of which we still see some impact into the 21st century. In India, this phenomenon of recording technology came in an amazingly short time after the introduction of the technique in the USA and Europe, thereby opening up a new range of possibilities in the field of music. The sudden and dramatic impact of new technology enabled new forms of production, dissemination, circulation and consumption of music. Early recording, made primarily on flat discs made of hard shellac or, in some cases, cardboard, was rudimentary in its techniques. The recording instruments were brought from Europe or the United States, and in the earliest stages so were the recording blanks. Recording was done in informal surroundings: at hotels or the houses of wealthy patrons; later, there were recording camps set up in villages or small towns where artistes congregated. The recordists had little understanding of the sounds they were recording.

This was the first fascinating encounter between technology and music. The vocalists took on the challenge put forth by this new technology of presenting their work in approximately three minutes – this, given the innately improvisatory nature of Indian music. The scratchy and seemingly garbled sounds that opne hears from the earliest surviving gramophone discs speak to us eloquently over the passage of a century telling us an important story.

" These Machines Talk, Sing, Recite, Play Bands, Orchestras. They permanently record human voices and reproduce them naturally."

"The Phonograph", ad by Paul & Sons, *Indian Mirror*, 1899

India is a peculiar country in respect of language. To overcome this challenge, regional language-based music became an important part of the marketing strategy of the recording companies. This strategy was well received and the subsequent recordings duly targeted this diversity. The gramophone industry spread in both North and South India rapidly and prolifically. This book is an account of the phenomenon in North India.

Women in the 78 RPM gramophone era made a significant contribution to Indian art, music and literature, and were involved in theatre and film. They have had a profound influence on subsequent performance music. Ironically, there is little available in the public memory about the *gaanewalis* or songstresses; this is a legacy that has largely been preserved through the gramophone records that first made their appearance in India in the first decade of the 20th century. Collectors estimate that the number of records issued in India would amount to about half a million – a large corpus of which remains unheard and inaccessible to contemporary audiences.

Even though *baijis*, or singing ladies, were important to the world of performance, they were perhaps not really a part of the mainstream discussion and discourse on music in India. While it is estimated in discographies that over 500 women were recorded in different regional languages all over India, little is known about these artistes. Gramophone companies, initially run by Americans and Europeans and not by upper-caste Indians, actively recruited *baijis* for their early recordings.

The gramophone record revolutionized the ways in which music was heard, and gradually also started to craft new social norms. For one, the commercial success of the record made this avenue an attractive option for many musicians, both performers and accompanists. Those among them who became celebrities were clearly affluent and lived posh lifestyles, but there were also those who died in penury. This was also the time of the nationalist movement – a struggle against foreign rule, but also a movement with a reformist agenda. The *baijis'* profession was condemned and they were branded as 'loose women'. Many of them then moved to the theatre and films, given their understanding of the social stigmas faced by their community, and sensing the opportunity encoded in cinema for a potential career change. Some – like Jaddan Bai, better known as film actress Nargis' mother – moved from being successful and respected performers to becoming film producers and actresses.

The voices of these women still speak to us, requiring us to imagine their historical contexts. There are many stories of struggle, courage and marginalization as *baijis* made history: from being mere entertainers to people who had generations of camp followers, creating the way for a new language in the performing arts for women performers in India. This book is a journey through the lives and music of these singing ladies who played an important role in the making of the entertainment industry of India – an industry that is celebrated the world over today.

TELEFUNKEN
TELEFUNKEN

THE BEGINNINGS OF Recording

The first recording machine to enter the Indian market was the phonograph, which was invented by Thomas Alva Edison in 1877. Maharaj Lal & Sons of Delhi began importing the wax cylinder machines in 1898. They soon became a fairly popular novelty among the 'native' elite. Colloquialisms sprang up to describe this western invention.

Early recordings were either instrumental pieces by western orchestras or songs in foreign languages. Therefore the machine remained but a curiosity for its many buyers. In Calcutta H. Bose, who ran a perfumery and a cycle hardware store, was the first to acquire dealership of Edison Phonographs. Others soon followed suit, and many Indian traders in different parts of the country opened up agencies for marketing phonographs manufactured by companies like Edison Records, Columbia and Pathe.

"As we steamed down the Channel into the unknown, I felt like Marco Polo starting out on his journeys."

Fred William Gaisberg (1873–1951)

The real breakthrough in sound recording came with the disc record, when the London-based Gramophone & Typewriter Ltd. (GTL), later renamed the Gramophone Company Ltd., decided to set up office in Calcutta in the year 1901. In July 1901, John Watson Hawd of GTL arrived in India to survey the local market. Hawd toured the cities of Calcutta, Bombay and Madras before setting up GTL's first store at Chowringhee Lane, Calcutta. Jamshedji Framji Madan of Corinthian Theatre and Amarendra Nath Dutta of Classic Theatre were contacted to arrange for local artistes as Hawd looked for suitable places to conduct recording sessions.

A year later Fred William Gaisberg, the sound engineer at GTL, began his expedition of the Far East with stops in Calcutta, Singapore, Hong Kong, Shanghai, Tokyo and Burma. Gaisberg and his assistant George Dillnut arrived on the shores of Calcutta aboard the "Coromandel" on 27 October 1902. With little knowledge of Indian genres and limited access to local artistes, the task that lay ahead was far from easy. Gaisberg soon recognized the taboos surrounding the singing

This page
Above: The Great Eastern Hotel, Calcutta

Facing page
Above: Dancing and singing troupe
Below: Nautch party
Courtesy: CIViC Archive, New Delhi

Dancing and Singing Party

Nautch Party.

No. 100 - Dancing girls with musicians - Jaipur
Gobind Ram & Oodey Ram, Jaipur.

DANCING GIRLS IN ATTITUDE.

profession and the ignorance of his English contacts at interpreting the local scene: "I discovered that the English, whom we contacted and who were acting as our agents and factors, might be living on another planet for all the interest they took in Indian music."

Despite the initial hurdles, the first recording with female artistes from Amarendra Dutta's Classic Theatre was held in a makeshift studio in Calcutta's Great Eastern Hotel. Gaisberg disapproved of their voices; as he wrote in his memoir:

"We made our first native records. Two little nautch girls (Soshi Mukhi and Fani Bala), 14 and 16, with miserable voices. They persisted in covering their faces and never got over the embarrassment we inspired."

But just three days later Gaisberg conducted the first recording with Gauhar Jan, the famed singer of Calcutta. Gauhar Jan amazed her audience both by the improvisations of her voice and her luxurious lifestyle:

"Calve came to our lab with far less cortege, and required much less attendants. The Mohammedan girl could lay considerable claim to coloratura voice."

She remained the mainstay of GTL's enterprise in the early years, recording over 400 songs in as many as twenty different languages, and was a key figure in the success of commercial sound recording in India.

Beginning with Calcutta, GTL's network spread to other major towns and cities of India including Bombay, Madras, Delhi, Benares and Lucknow. Other major recording labels like Beka, Odeon, Pathe and Twin soon formed associations with native businessmen to capitalize on the newly found market. From north to south, one recording expedition followed another, laying the early foundations of what was to later become the country's music industry.

In 1908, GTL set up the first record factory at 139 Beliaghata Road, Sealdah, Calcutta, to compensate for the falling supplies of mica and shellac in their foreign plants. Besides emerging as one of the biggest markets, India remained one of the largest exporters of vinyl records in the 20th century.

The first decade of the 20th century witnessed the establishment of a flourishing industry with a large number of companies, both native and European, engaged in selling commercially produced records, It has been observed that between 1899 and 1914, as many as 12 major recording corporations were operating in India at one time or the other, and at least 26 recording label found acceptance among the Indian audience.

Facing page
Above: Dancing girls with musicians, photograph by Gobind Ram and Oodey Ram Firm, Jaipur
Below: Dancing girls
Courtesy: CIViC Archive, New Delhi

This page
Above: A book illustration of Malka Jan *'Agrewali'*
Courtesy: SIRC, Mumbai

Below: An early advertisement for Edison Phonographs

WOMEN AND Recording

Several reasons contributed to a scenario where women singers became a preferred choice over their male counterparts. As music became available to the general public with the entry of the gramophone, there was no deciding as to who could or could not sing. Anybody who could learn and adapt found an audience. The courtesans had no reservations about sharing their repertoire. Since they were born entertainers, the recording industry represented just one more opportunity for them to reach out to more people: more than they could ever reach through their performances in courts or at *kothas*.

Coincidentally, even the technology at that time was more suited to recording feminine voices. The early recording machines were relatively less suitable for recording deep masculine voices. Hiring male artistes was hardly a profitable proposition, although some male artistes went so far as to imitate the feminine voice signature by trying to sing in a higher pitch. Peara Saheb, who for a short time served as a court musician to Nawab Wajid Ali Shah, was among the few male artistes to have sung for recording companies in the initial years, and he had a peculiar feminine voice.

The recording companies were typically capitalistic enterprises looking to expand their market. And the engineers were in a way indifferent to the taboos surrounding the profession of courtesans and more interested in the popularity their singing enjoyed among the Indian masses. Refusal on the part of singers who practised classical music drove gramophone agents to explore the possibilities manifested in the fascinating world of *kothas*.

But what really made the courtesans stand out was how well they adapted to the opportunities offered by this medium. Women artistes made remarkable use of the potential of the music industry, often creating new images of themselves; and, at the same time, also recasting classical and light music. The catalogues of early recordings show the variety of music that was generated: classical and semi-classical music, instrumental music, religious recitations, parodies, comic skits and even animal imitations.

The variety of genres covered was also complemented by the linguistic competence exhibited by many women artistes. Gauhar Jan from Calcutta is said to have recorded in over ten different languages.

As professional singers the women were often dependent upon their male patrons, but records provided them with new avenues of self-expression. Their voices could finally reach the drawing rooms of those who could not come to their salons to attend *soirées*. Records were their way around societal taboos.

Fame achieved through the gramophone seems to have redeemed their talent, providing them with bigger platforms and a popularity that was unheard of at that time among musicians. The companies singled out individual singers, comedians and theatre artistes, and selected their most popular songs for recording. These stars seem to have been better known and more popular than any Hollywood or Indian silent film stars of those days.

"Gramophone fame", as it was referred to at the time, was achieved, in part, through a concerted publicity and marketing campaign on

> I met the lady (Gauhar Jan) at our laboratory when she came to sing, and was impressed by her sharpness. She sings in some 20 languages including Hindustani, Turkish, Bengali, Katchi, Gujarati and Telugu.
>
> Fred William Gaisberg

Facing page
Above: Peara Saheb
Courtesy: K.K. Rastogi Collection, Varanasi

This page
Left: Miss Charutara
Above: Miss Dalimmoni
Courtesy: Ashish Bhadra, Kolkata

behalf of the record companies. For example, women artistes figured prominently and widely in the print media. Advertised and featured in the popular press, pictures of these new singing stars were reproduced in numerous publications including songbooks, newspapers, journals and posters. This helped to transform stage performers into a new kind of gramophone recording stars with greatly expanded audiences beyond the face-to-face relationship of a live performance.

The newly found wealth and prestige was crucial as larger numbers of women artistes throughout India bagged exclusive contracts with multiple recording company labels simultaneously. The gramophone years provided a precedent for the entry of many women singers into cinema and later radio. The popularity they achieved also laid the groundwork for ticketed live concerts in the following decades, something that was unheard of in the time of court performances. That general audiences were willing to watch them sing was no small feat given the taboos around the singing profession in the 1900s. Without doubt the early talkie era in films owes significantly to the tradition of women singers who fearlessly and successfully made this transition, taking on a variety of roles ranging from singing, acting, directing and composing to producing features under their own banners.

Most importantly, records for the first time laid the foundations of a female bastion in Indian music culture, which served as an inspiration for generations of women to follow and learn from.

The genres recorded on gramophone:

Dhrupad, Dhamar, Sadra, Khayal, Chaturang, Tarana, Sargam-geet, Thumri, Dadra, Sohar, Bandra, Ghato, Chaiti, Saavan, Jhoola.

Also represented were Ghazals and Geets, and various kinds of devotional music including Kirtan, Bhajan, Qawwali, Marsiya and Soz.

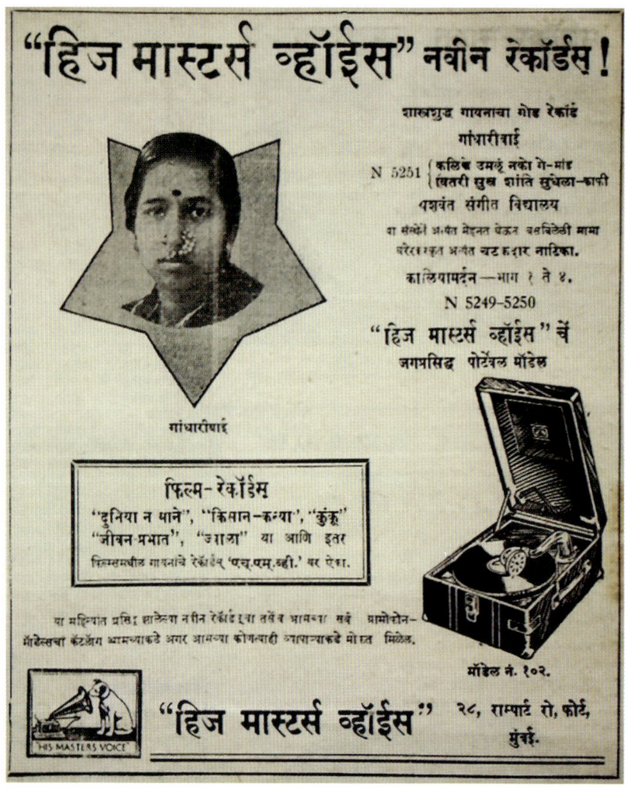

This page
Above: Miss Manodasundari
Courtesy: Ashish Bhadra, Kolkata

Right: An HMV advertisement for a Marathi recording artiste
Courtesy: SIRC, Mumbai

Facing page
Miss K.B. Sundarambal in front of the microphone at the Columbia Studio Hollway's gardens, October 1932
Courtesy: The Hindu Archives

In Conversation:

Girija Devi

A renowned classical vocalist from the Banaras *gharana*, Girija Devi has contributed enormously to the Hindustani musical repertoire over the years. Known as the 'Queen of Thumri' among admirers for her phenomenal innovations in the Thumri style of singing and its mainstreaming, she has taken Indian music to many national and international platforms. A Padma Shri, Padma Bhushan and Padma Vibhushan awardee, she is also a recipient of the prestigious Tansen Award. Here she shares some personal anecdotes about her life in music and meaningful insights into the Hindustani music culture.

Unconventional Beginnings...

My father was extremely fond of music. And my initial introduction to singing was through him. I started learning music under late Pandit Sarju Prasad Misra ji. He really admired how I took to learning music. But he was equally apprehensive about teaching female students since many would eventually get married and not take up music as a profession.

As I began taking lessons, this is what I wanted to change. He would come to our house to teach because women were not allowed to go out much during those times.

I worked in my first film when I was just nine. One of my uncles was a wrestler in Calcutta. In those days *akhadas*, or arenas, were places full of activity. Film directors often frequented the *akhadas* to find wrestlers for action sequences in their films. One of the directors asked my uncle if I would like to act in a film since he knew that I could sing too. That is how I landed my first role in a film called *Yaad Rahe*. It was produced by a Mr. Kumar, and the director, Mr. Moolchandani, was a Sindhi.

In those days they would hang the microphone above us, and as we moved, it would move along. That's how things were recorded then. The musicians would sit close by on *chowkies* and the music director would coordinate everything. The recordings were very spontaneous, unlike playback singing today where everything can be edited later.

Since cinema had not quite become the industry it is today, we never really thought of collecting photographs or posters of the film. Now hardly anything remains from my first film as most of the souvenirs have got misplaced over the years.

My Guruji was furious when he found out that I had been working in films. And he literally scolded my father for letting me work in the industry. The times were different then and people did not think the same way about women working in the film industry as they do today.

After this incident, Guruji persuaded my entire family to come to Banaras which is where I resumed my *taleem*.

Jaddan 'Khan'

Jaddan Bai was an amazing singer and she had a charming personality. My father and she trained under the same Guru. And that's how they knew each other. I used to call her *bua* (aunt).

Jaddan Bai's daughter Nargis and I grew up together. We would practise and play together while my father was taking his lessons. Nargis grew up to become an actress, while I chose music as my profession.

When it came to the singing repertoire, Jaddan Bai had a range that was matched by only a few of her contemporaries. She was known for graceful renditions of Khayal, Thumri and Tappa. People would often address her as Jaddan 'Khan' instead of Jaddan Bai, because she knew as much as the male artistes of her time.

The Importance of Listening

I grew up listening to the likes of Gauhar Jan, Jaddan Bai, Siddheshwari Devi, Badi Moti Bai and Heera Bai, Abdul Karim Khan Saheb, Ustad Faiyaaz Khan Sahib, Pandit Omkarnath Thakur, Ustad Amir Saheb, Bade Ghulam Ali Saheb – many of these singers were available on record by that time. Some I got to listen to during their concerts.

This was a time before the Partition happened. There were singers like Nazakat Salamat and Roshanara Begum who later moved to Pakistan. These were the singers I grew up with.

Mehfils used to happen but the singers would also visit each other's houses frequently. It was a closely knit community. There was no cinema in those days; the only exposure to music was through people we knew. Colleges came up later, but to listen to those singers was something that is hard to find a substitute for even today.

The Universities

The music scenario did not change overnight, but with the coming of music universities, the situation changed drastically for women in particular. In Maharashtra, women from renowned families started learning music. In Gujarat, Mrinalini Sarabhai, who hailed from a prestigious background, began performing Bharatanatyam on public platforms.

When women from respectable families started learning music in these universities and institutions, the society's way of viewing singers and specially women artistes underwent a change. I am talking of a period merely eighty years before today. So, in my time, as women started learning "publicly", our performances were no longer seen as vulgar.

Photos courtesy: Parthiv Shah

JAN, BAI, DEVI AND More

The names of *tawaifs* or professional singers often carried with them the titles which, at the time, defined their identities. For instance, there was Gauhar 'Jan', Zohra 'Bai', 'Miss' Fani Bala and so on. The unconventional and textured lives of these professional women artistes have been a matter of both curiosity and controversy.

Historically, the *tawaif* tradition was made up of multifarious groups from various regions of northern India. These singing and dancing troupes were either named after their communities or the arts they practised: for example, the *Nats* of Uttar Pradesh, a nomadic tribe that excels in dancing and jugglery, or the temple dancers of South India, namely the *Devadasis*. *Kasbi*, *Bai*, *Nachaniya* and *Kanchani* – over the years, the significance of their professional and artistic origins was lost and the groups were brought under a consolidated "branding".

More so during the decades of British colonization that led to new-founded notions of morality among the reform-minded upper and middle-class Indians, women performers were generalized as courtesans and, unfortunately, even became synonymous with commonplace 'prostitutes' in the era of the country's Independence.

It is a rather misguided belief that these women entertainers were mainly Muslim courtesans: a popular misunderstanding probably attributable to the time of Mughal rule when the *tawaif* culture was popularized in India as well as the Arabic roots of the Urdu word *tawaif*.

Historically, in the early years of the 19th century, mention of both Hindu and Muslim courtesans is found in all the important trading cities and imperial centres of North India. Cities and towns like Calcutta, Bombay, Delhi, Banaras, Lucknow, Kanpur, Agra and Jaipur were places of remarkable cultural activity. Five distinct categories of Muslim courtesans recorded were *Kanchani*, *Ramjani*, *Samat*, *Hurkini* and *Maljadi*. They were distinguished by their singing and dancing talent as well as the communities they came from.

Similarly the Hindu courtesans had distinctive groups, namely *Patar*, *Pahadi Patar*, *Devadasi*, *Domni*, *Goegirni*, *Perni*, *Natini* and *Gandharvini*. The *Gandharvini*, *Patar*, *Devadasi* and *Goegirni* are said to have belonged to a higher status. Some of the *Natinis* embraced Islam but they had clan distinctions similar to the Hindu *Natinis*.

Most of the courtesan families came from nomadic North Indian tribes and were generically addressed as *deras* (singular: *dera*). The *deras* were mobile encampments that moved from city to city entertaining the populace. The leading courtesans of these troupes, called *deredars*, were singers of great repute. Girls who depended on the *deredar* were called 'nautch' girls.

It is believed that salons or *kothas*, the permanent dwellings of courtesan families, were partly an outcome of the decline of the Mughal empire. *Kothas* were large establishments with complex

Facing page and this page
From the "Beauties of Lucknow" series
by Darogah Abbas Ali
Courtesy: Anil Relia Archives, Ahmedabad

Next two pages
Stereographic photograph of professional dancing girls in the streets of Old Delhi
by H.C. White
Courtesy: Anil Relia Archives, Ahmedabad

The "PERFECT" STEREOGRAPH. (Trade Mark.)
EDITION de LUXE. Patented April 14, 1908.
Professional dancing girls in the streets of old Delhi, India.

hierarchies among the women performers. Socially and professionally, *tawaifs* distinguished themselves not only from prostitutes, but also from other professional female performing artistes like Natnis or acrobats/singers/dancers, and Nautanki Bais or folk theatre actresses, by their performance context. A *tawaif*'s performance was sponsored and witnessed by the nobility and the elite either in the royal court or a *kotha*, as opposed to a performance in the street witnessed by the common public.

Within the musicians community, the standard hierarchy consisted of the Bai, those who sing, at the top; followed by Jan, or those who sing and dance. After this comes Kanij, broadly defined as 'entertainers', and finally, Khanagi, those who included sexual favours as part of the entertainment package.

Women from singing communities whose families resided in Goa and the Maharashtra region, and who were trained as professional performers in dance and music, were known by the names Kalavant, Naikin, Bhavin and Murli. Kalavant and Naikin were synonymous expressions used for castes and classes of hereditary musicians whose origin was in Goa.

This page and facing page
From the "Beauties of Lucknow" series by Darogah Abbas Ali
Courtesy: Anil Relia Archives, Ahmedabad

To some, Naikin is similar to *Goekarin*, a term used for the class of singing women, but according to some other sources, early 20th century women singers from Goa considered the word 'Naikin' to be equivalent to prostitute and therefore avoided its use. Below Kalavantins and Naikins there were two other categories known as Bhavins and Murlis with Murlis placed at the bottom of the ladder. Kalavants or Naikins claim to be descendants from *apsaras* and *gandharvas*, and give proof of their connections with Hindu temples.

Interestingly, the titles also take on different meanings in different regions and their use becomes gendered. For instance, the word 'Kalavant' in North India is used for respectable hereditary male musicians specializing in vocal music who do not play the *tabla* or *sarangi*, whereas in Maharashtra and adjoining regions 'Kalavantin' is used for a dancing girl or courtesan. A further distinction has also been made between Kalavantin (a dancing girl) and Kasbin (a singing woman). The former dances and stands while singing, whereas the latter sits.

A microcosm of talent and entertainment, the world of Baijis has always been a complex territory defying shallow definitions and categorization by outsiders. Its richness may have withered with the ravages of time, but its intrigue is everlasting.

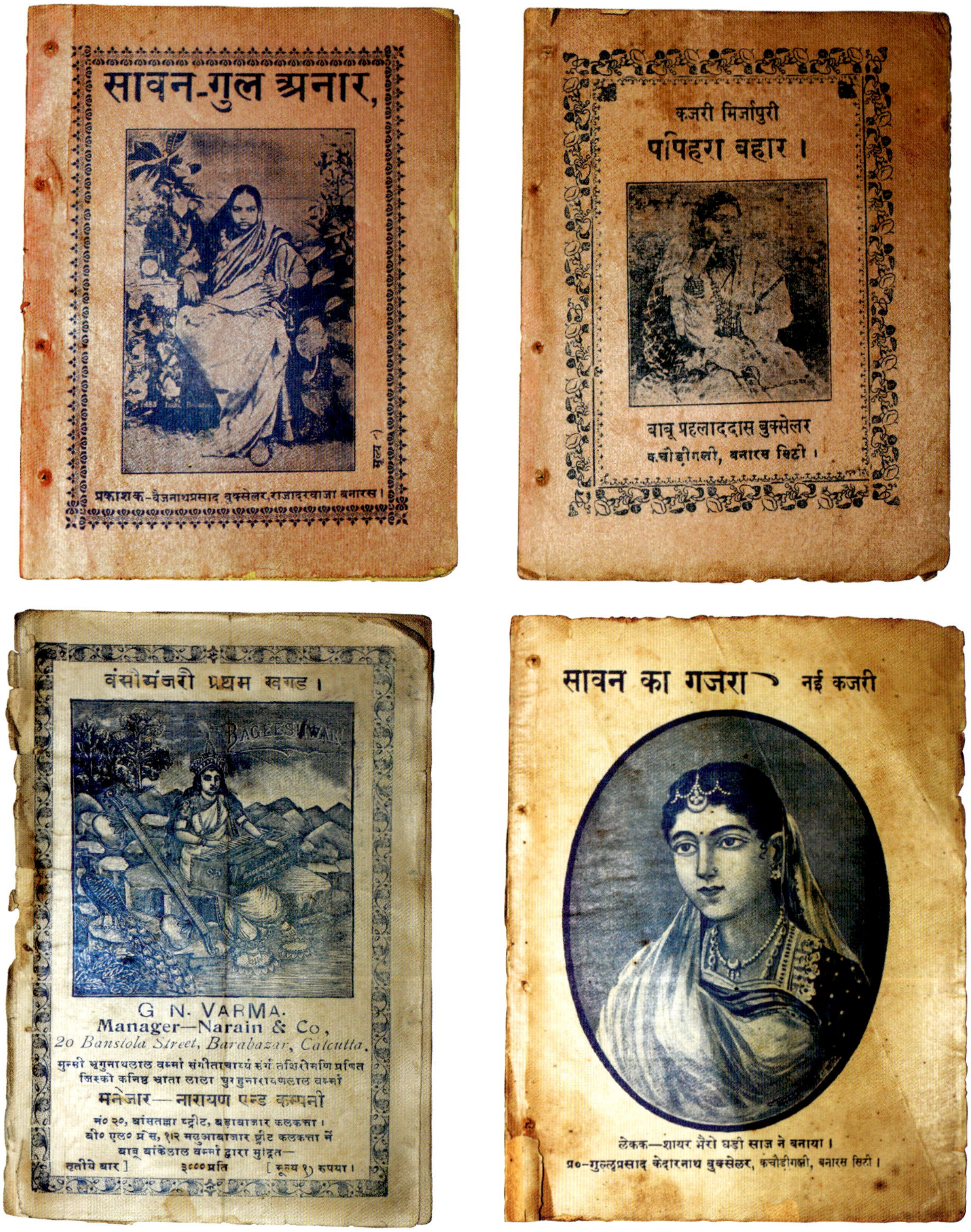

This page
Booklets of popular musical genres
Courtesy: K.K. Rastogi Collection, Varanasi

Facing page
From the "Beauties of Lucknow" series
by Darogah Abbas Ali
Courtesy: Anil Relia Archives, Ahmedabad

THE IMPACT OF Technology

When recording technology was first brought to India in the early years of the twentieth century, it was welcomed with a similar admixture of fascination and distrust as was the telegraph a few decades ago. Some in the artiste fraternity were charmed by the magical prospects of this western novelty while others were suspicious of its 'unworldly' prowess.

Afraid of losing their singing talent, many *gharanedars* chose not to lend their voices to the records. Some also feared the "vulgar" publicizing of their artistic endeavours among sections they disapproved of. For instance, Ziauddin Khan, uncle of Ustad Nasir Aminuddin Dagar, did not commit to recording because he would not profane his art by making it available to "any common courtesan" who could afford to buy a record.

Enayet Khan used to announce his name as Prof. Enayet Khan Sitariya. Vilayat Khan announced his name by saying that he was Enayat's son. Interestingly, in one of the recordings Enayet Khan ends his rendering by saying: "Prof. Enayet Khan Sitariye, Vilayet Khan ke baap!"

Those who accepted the technology had to mould their singing to the demands of this new medium. Perhaps the greatest challenge for the early recording artistes was the provision of the 3-minute rule. A recording disc could only carry 3 minutes of music. The limit imposed was rather unusual for singers who were used to performing in courts and *mehfils* where anything but time would have been a constraint. Practised in the techniques of improvisation and spontaneity of the classical tradition, the pioneering artistes soon found ways to bring the aura of the *mehfil* into the drawing rooms of the commonplace audience. In her recording of *Raag Gandhari*, Gauhar Jan, the first artiste to record commercially, begins the rhythmic composition at a faster tempo, perhaps being over-conscious of the time factor, but then cleverly slows down to suit the composition and the time-frame. Zohra Bai Agrewali (1868–1913), the fabulous Khayal singer, came to be greatly admired among artistes and connoisseurs alike for her perfect renditions in the 3-minute format.

With the arrival of double-sided 78 rpm discs, many vocalists and instrumentalists further improvised to record the non-rhythmic *alap* on one side and the rhythmic part on the other: a convention that continued into the cassette culture that made its entry towards the end of the twentieth century.

The atmosphere of the *mehfil* was recreated in the studio as people were brought in to exclaim their admiration during the recording. More importantly, as musical pieces turned into packaged commodities, the selection of genres became as much a matter of popular appeal as of the ease of adapting a genre to the 3-minute rule. The first half of the 20th century saw a series of semi-classical and light classical genres being marketed under Hindustani classical titles, and regional genres like Kajri, Chaiti and Thumri became a rage within the recording circles. It has been observed that the more traditional forms, like Dhrupad and Dhamar, constituted only a negligible portion of the recorded repertoire.

An interesting practice that was born out of the constraints of production was that of the singers having to announce their names at the end of the recording. Since the records were initially sent to Hanover, Germany for pressing, this ensured that the names of the

Artistes who recorded: Ustad Allauddin Khan, Ustad Abdul Karim Khan, Peara Saheb

Those who resisted: Pandit Vishnu Digambar Paluskar, Bhaskarbuwa Bakhale, Ustad Alladiya Khan

Women artistes who recorded very little: Kesar Bai Kerkar, Babli Bai Salgaonkar

This page
Top to bottom: Alladiya Khan, Abdul Karim Khan, Kesar Bai Kerkar

Facing page
Above: Bhaskarbuwa Bakhale

artistes were not mixed. This also probably addressed the problem of piracy. These announcements however disappeared when GTL opened its first factory in Sealdah, Calcutta. The locals working there called it the factory the *Baja Khana*.

The early recording contraptions also placed significant limitations on "who or what" was being recorded. Having to sing into the horn of the phonograph, vocalists were bound to limit their natural head movements. For instrumentalists, though the ordeal was different, it was nonetheless as severe. Barring a few instruments like the *shehnai* or the clarinet, it was almost impossible to position the phonograph for recording a range of Hindustani instruments.

The early forties saw a shift in the outlook of artistes towards recording. Being recorded began to be considered the most prestigious thing that could happen to a performer. By the 1940s and 1950s opportunities and openings to record for commercial companies and the radio came to be universally sought after, even though the format that recording studios demanded of musicians was strange and inhospitable. The physical placing of percussion instruments and other accompaniments naturally gave precedence to the requirements of electronics, rather than to the accustomed rapport between the musicians which is the life of any performance. It was a daunting experience, if not an ordeal, for a singer to sit far away from his *tabla* and *sarangi*, and still be able to warm up as in a live concert. But this was one uncomfortable situation most of the artistes resigned themselves to, in the hope of larger audiences and immortality. In any case, from being something new-fangled that

was resisted on principle, recording became the new status symbol and introduced a shift in traditional attitudes towards classical music.

The gramophone transformed listening habits as it normalized the repetition of listening. Records became newfound sources of inspiration for the next generation of musicians. Their first lessons came engraved on the grooves of 78 rpm discs, and the attendance of live performances followed. Listening to and copying somebody else's style emerged as a new form of education. Later, both the composition and style of an artiste were looked back at from earlier recordings of the maestros of the *gharana* or tradition they represented. As preservation was instated through gramophone records, the idea of ephemerality espoused earlier by *mehfils* was pushed to the front by the very technologies that would appear to have eliminated it. So, live concerts once again became important because of their temporal experience of momentariness.

बाबा पुर्बी धुन मा गावे
बेटा फिल्मी गीत सुनावे
घर मा बाजे ग्रामुफून
आधा फागुन आधा जून

Father sings to Eastern tunes,
And the son hums the songs from films.
In the house plays the gramophone,
Through December, and all through June

Ameer Jan Siddheshwari Devi

Zohra Bai

Gauhar Jan Rasoolan Bai

Mohammad Ban

Janki Bai Girindra Kumari Doanni Jan

Begum Akhtar Dasi Guljar Beg

Roshanara Begum Angurabala

Kusum Kumari Kumu

Mehboob Jan Sholapur Radha Bai Coimbatore

Deen Bai Kasturi Fatarfekarin Miss Gafoora

Hingan Bai Jarao Jan Malka Jan Bai

Dhanakoti Sardari F

Jadumani Dasi Indubala Kali Jan

Menka Shirodkar

Mehboob Jan Gangu Bai Hangal Kiti Jan Alla Bandi Buri

Bhuvaneshwari

Munni Jan Jorbanu Bhavani Ashgari Jan

Mahamuda Jan Giribala Dasi Achhan Bai Vahid Jan

Bedana Dasi Jarupiya Jan Manada Sundari Dasi Sunder Ja

Papa Jan Purnakumari Dasi

Mushtari Bai Miss Kallo Zeba

Mumtaz Jan Husna Jan

Piyari Jan Mah

Miss Godavari Miss Jumma

Nawab Jan Krishni Jhulpavali Jawahir Bai M

Nazirjan Panna Pratibha Dasi

SINGING Sensations

Music in India has always evolved in the context of distinct social and religious customs. Be it the classical genres or the regional styles, our songs have always reflected the way people lived, their desires and devotion, their love and emotions. Over the years, these contexts have been lost to the general public. Some of the *baijis* managed to negotiate these complex dynamics, and went on to become famous artistes through a combination of skill, training and versatility.

The oldest surviving form of the Indian classical music, the Dhrupad, developed primarily as a form of worship in which offerings are made to the divine through *naad* (the sound). Dhrupad itself is said to have descended from a form known as *Prabandh*, a fixed composition with a beginning and an end, set to a particular *raag*.

With the need to relate to a wider audience and listenership, another form, the Dhamar, evolved. Contrary to the austerity of the Dhrupad, Dhamar was a livelier style. Today, Dhamar is considered a relatively light and romantic musical form, which is sung during the festival of Holi, in the season of spring.

However, by the mid-19th century, *Khayal Gayaki* had eclipsed Dhrupad as the preferred style of performance in the courts. The term *khayal* comes from the Urdu word *'kheyal'*, meaning 'imagination' or 'thought'. With the development of the Khayal, love became a predominant theme in Indian vocal music. The sensuality of emotions was perfectly captured by the Thumri, which became a generic name even for forms such as the Dadra, Chaiti and Hori. The word *thumri* comes from the Hindi colloquialism *'thumkana'*, referring to a sensuous and attractive gait. Indian socio-cultural history testifies to the intimate bond between *tawaifs* and the musical arts. Thumri as a genre was widely appropriated and popularized by the *tawaif* culture in North India.

Malika Pukhraj, popular Ghazal and folk singer, advocated that these women should not be called *tawaifs*. Instead they should be called *baijis*.

Historically, music education in India for a long time was based on the oral tradition. That is, knowledge was passed from the Guru or teacher to the *shishyas* or disciples orally. It is known that since the *guru–shishya parampara* was largely a male domain, *tawaifs* wanting to learn music had to pay exorbitantly high fees. However, despite the societal constraints, these women were able to make their presence felt and contribute substantially to the social history of music in India. Even male *ustads* looked up to them for their mastery of Hindustani musical styles and singing.

The early years of the gramophone era were a period of transition for this community of women; a transition from being court performers to being 'singing sensations' for more general audiences. And it was from this period of transition that the idea of *baijis* came to be.

Gauhar Jan

The First Diva

Gauhar Jan was one of 20th-century India's greatest performing artistes. She was Calcutta's best known courtesan who, in 1902, became the first classical singer to record for England's Gramophone Company. In fact, the very first record released in India was a Khayal composition in *Raag Jogiya* sung by her.

Born in Azamgarh, located in present-day Uttar Pradesh, Gauhar Jan was an Anglo-Indian, which was not unusual for a *tawaif* in the early 1900s. But her ancestry was uncommon on various other counts. Christened Eileen Angelina at birth, her parents were Robert Yeoward, an Anglo-Armenian, and Adeline Victoria, who had a Hindu mother and a Jewish-English father. Adeline Victoria was herself an accomplished singer as well as a fine poet. After Adeline parted ways with her husband who had little appreciation for her musical talent, she went to Banaras, converted to Islam and took on the name Malka Jan. Her daughter was renamed Gauhar. There is speculation as to whether Gauhar's maternal grandmother, Rukmini, was also a courtesan. If true, this would establish Gauhar as part of a *tawaif* lineage as was usually the case.

Gauhar made her musical debut at the age of 13 and was soon counted among the best singers of her time. It was popularly sai, *"Gauhar ke bina mehfil / jaise shaadi ke bina dulhan."* A disciple of the celebrated Bindadin Maharaj (Birju Maharaj's grandfather), she was also an accomplished dancer known for her *abhinaya*. And, like her mother, an excellent poet as well.

Gauhar Jan was known for her experimental approach to music; she borrowed freely from various *gharanas* as and when she thought fit. She had a scintillating personality, the very stuff of star quality, which never failed to impress. Extraordinarily sensitive, she had the ability to rapidly gauge the taste and mood of her audience, and adapt her performance accordingly. Once, during a performance in Bombay, she spontaneously regaled her audience with *Natya Sangeet* in Marathi. And she had been singing *Rabindra Sangeet* to Bengali audiences long before its crystallization into a genre.

Between 1902 and 1920, Gauhar Jan recorded over 200 songs on 78 rpm discs for various gramophone labels in over ten languages, including French, Arabic, Pushto and Tamil. Her discs cover the entire range of Indian musical genres from Dhrupad and Khayal to the Bhajan, apart from the *tawaif*'s usual repertory of Thumri, Dadra and the like.

Being the first classical artiste to record, it fell upon her to adapt the *raag* to the required 3-minute format. That she accomplished this successfully attests not only to her musical genius, but also to her audacity. Gauhar established a template for those after her to follow. For this reason alone, her discs constitute a pioneering contribution to the Indian recording industry.

This page
Above: Gauhar Jan
Courtesy: SIRC, Mumbai

Facing page
Above: Gauhar Jan's sketch on a matchbox label
Courtesy: CIViC Archives, New Delhi

Below: Gauhar Jan at a recording session
Courtesy: SIRC, Mumbai

Gauhar was a celebrity, a diva even. Matchboxes made in Austria and selling in India at the time carried her picture on their labels, and her photograph was featured on postcards across the country. Despite protests from a puritanical middle class, she, together with her contemporary Janki Bai, was chosen by the British authorities to perform at King George V's coronation at the famous Delhi Durbar of 1911. Gauhar was at the peak of her career at this time. She owned properties and cars, and was in the habit of taking rides across the city of Calcutta in a four horse-drawn carriage, flouting the British rules which forbade this. Known for never repeating her flamboyant outfits and for showing off her expensive diamond jewellery, Gauhar was the highest paid artiste of her time, charging Rs. 1000 per concert.

Apart from being a successful *tawaif*, Gauhar was also a serious classical musician. V.N. Bhatkhande, the foremost theoretician of Hindustani classical music, has paid tribute to her as one of the country's best Khayal singers. Describing one of her performances, eminent musicologist D.P. Mukherjee said: "She sang a Dhrupad in *Adana*, a Dadra in the same *raag*. And yet a third Khayal in *Adana*. Since then, I have found it difficult to concentrate on *Adana* even when it is sung by the best in the country."

Gauhar Jan's career straddled a time when India was undergoing a transformation, and the tradition of the *tawaif* as a cultural and historical persona was slowly fading away. The movement for Indian independence was gathering steam and the western-educated middle classes, having imbibed the notion of democratic nationhood, were fleshing out the concept of a national culture. Indian music entered into this project of course. But the nationalist agenda was underpinned by a middle-class morality which appropriated the *tawaif*'s music while leaving the *tawaif* herself out in the cold. In fact the first Home Ministry of independent India went so far as to ban *tawaifs* from singing on All India Radio by stipulating that only married women were eligible to perform.

Gauhar, however, seemed to have moved with the times. She was recording for several companies, and performed in *mehfils* as well as ticketed concerts open to the public with equal ease. Her private life, on the other hand, proved to be a bigger challenge.

In 1925, towards the end of her recording career, Gauhar found patronage at the Rampur court and then with bourgeois patrons in the city of Bombay. Musically, she was as brilliant and accomplished as ever. In 1927, while at Rampur, she performed for Lord Irwin, the newly appointed Viceroy of India, and subsequently gave several excellent performances in Bombay.

In 1928, Gauhar Jan was appointed official musician to the court of Mysore. Though she performed there just thrice during the course of one-and-a-half years, it is reported that these performances were executed with her usual brilliance and flamboyance. She was plagued by poor health in Mysore and suffered frequent bouts of depression. On 17 January 1930, at the age of 57, Gauhar Jan passed away after a brief illness in a Mysore hospital. In the ensuing years she faded from public memory and her musical legacy faded into obscurity. Of this legacy, 150 records and a few photographs still exist, however, preserved by dedicated collectors.

Zohra Bai Agrewali

The Voice of Khayal on 78 RPMs

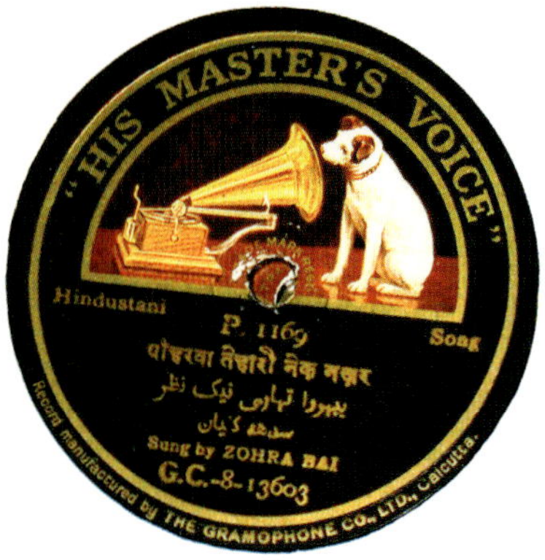

Like many of her contemporaries, Zohra Bai's life and illustrious music career has been put together from anecdotes about her performances and the memoirs of musicians and musical enthusiasts. The talented harmonium player and music composer Govindrao Sadashiv Tembe, and renowned singer of the Gwalior Gharana Ramkrishna Narhar Vaze, both admiringly mention her many concerts and the quality of her singing. Only a single photograph of her – with a *tanpura* and a child on her lap – survives, and there are doubts about its authenticity. To this day it is unclear if she got her surname due to her association with the Agra style of singing or because she spent a major part of her life in Agra.

Zohra Bai received her first lessons in music from her father Ahmad Khan, who was both an accomplished singer and an expert *sarangi* player. Later, she began her formal training under Mehboob Khan of Atrauli Gharana and Kale Khan of Mathura. As per the traditions of her time, Zohra was both a trained singer and a dancer, and her concerts were hugely popular in many princely states among rich and wealthy patrons. An expert Khayal singer, she was known for her expertise in rendering very fast and sharp *taans*.

In 1908, due to her widespread popularity, the Gramophone Company signed an exclusive contract with Zohra Bai on the condition that she would not sing for other recording labels. She was paid a sum of Rs. 2500 for 25 recordings in a year. At that time she was living in Patna where the Company did not have a recording studio. It is believed that the Company paid travel expenses for the entire troupe to attend recording sessions in other cities – proof of both her popularity and talent.

The recordings were held in the cities of Calcutta, Lucknow and Delhi, in hotels and makeshift studios. Those were the days when the master records were taken back to Hanover in Germany before the recordings were released in the market. Tragically, Zohra Bai passed away in 1913, months before her recordings were introduced in India. But over the years her recordings have surprised listeners and connoisseurs alike for the sheer ingenuity of her adaptation to the 3-minute rule. She had a range equalled by only a few of her contemporaries.

Between 1908 and 1911, Zohra Bai recorded over sixty songs on 78 rpm discs. Though relatively small in number, her recordings were best-sellers for many years to follow and her singing an inspiration to fellow-musicians.

Janki Bai Allahabadi

The Entrepreneur

Born in Banaras in 1880, Janki Bai was a popular and talented singer who went by the intriguing moniker *Chhappan Chhurivali* (one with 56 scars). Many interesting anecdotes recount the reasons for this rather unusual alias. According to one, she adopted the name after she was attacked by a jealous ruffian during one of her performances, and the 56 scars she received got her the title *Chhappan Chhurivali.*

Janki Bai belonged to the 'Vaggeyakar' community – a community of people who write, compose and sing songs. Janki was just a child when her father Shiv Balakram, a wrestler of the 'Ahir' caste, decided to abandon his family. In order to cope with the ensuing life of poverty, Janki's mother, Manaki, sold all her belongings and went to Allahabad, where she eventually became a courtesan. Janki's musical talents were nurtured under Ustad Hassu Khan, a pioneer of the Gwalior Gharana from Lucknow, who became her teacher on a handsome salary of Rs. 2000 per month. An accomplished artist, she was adept not only in singing, but also in writing verse and composing music. A collection of her songs has been published as a book under the title *Diwan-e-Janki.*

Janki Bai's singing became fairly popular among aristocratic circles in Allahabad and surrounding areas, and she performed frequently in many princely states of North India. She was a known contemporary and good friend of Gauhar Jan; and the duo were invited to sing together on King George V's visit to Allahabad . The popularity of Janki's performances soon won her a contract with the Gramophone Company. It is believed that between 1907 and 1929, she cut over 250 songs on 10-inch shellac 78 rpm discs in a range of popular and regional genres.

Janki Bai was famous for her effortless renditions of *raags* and light classical genres like Dadra, Hori, Kajri, Chaiti, Bhajan and Ghazal. Her foray into gramophone recording brought her attention from music lovers of the country. While she had begun recording for a sum of merely Rs. 250 for 20 songs, due to her popularity the fee escalated to as much as Rs. 5000 for 20 songs. It is said that roads leading to the record shops would get blocked by lovers of her music whenever a new stock of discs arrived. Many of her records sold over 25,000 copies, something unheard of till then even for highly accomplished singers of her time.

Surshri Kesar Bai Kerkar

The Voice of the Century

She came, she sang, she conquered. This is how every performance of Kesar Bai Kerkar came to be described. A singing diva, Kesar Bai was known for her clear voice and astute understanding of the rarest *raags*. Her music has become an ideal model for many women singers of today. Kesar Bai hailed from the community of Goekarins, women musicians associated with temples in Goa. Born in 1892 at Querim (Keri) in a family that earned a living through music, she received her first lessons within the community. Her formal *taleem* began at the age of 12, under Kirana maestro Abdul Karim Khan in Kolhapur. Later she also learnt under the musical legends Pandit Bhaskar Boa Bakhale and Barkatulla Khan.

In 1912 Kesar Bai began learning under Ustad Alladiya Khan, the founding father of the prestigious Jaipur–Atrauli Gharana. But after a brief period of just four months, Khan Sahib refused to continue with Kersar Bai as his disciple. Around 1913, when Pundit Bhaskar Bakhale left for Pune to handle the affairs of the Bharat Sangeet Sabha, Kesar Bai approached Shahu Maharaj, the ruler of Kolhapur, where Alladiya Saheb was a court musician. Finally, with the efforts and persuasion of her patrons Seth Vitthaldas and Gopaldas of Bombay, Alladiya Khan agreed to teach her, but he imposed a list of strict conditions and a hefty fee of Rs. 200 per month. Beginning in 1920, for the next ten years, Kesar Bai remained under Khan Sahib's tutelage and often shared the stage with him during concerts. She not only became one of the most refined voices of the Jaipur–Atrauli Gharana, but also one of the most respected performers in musical conferences held throughout India.

Kesar Bai had a melodious, luminous and sonorous voice, which could swoop down from a remarkable *taar-saptak* to a deep, resonant *mandra-saptak* uniformly and loud enough to be heard without a microphone. It is said that she often insisted on removing the microphone from stage. Some of her old admirers also claim that she had a very sharp memory and could easily identify her good listeners among the audience, wherever they sat during her performance. An astute performer, sometimes she would deliberately take a wrong note, a *swaravarjit*, to test her audience.

In 1965, to the surprise of the entire music fraternity and her admirers, Kesar Bai voluntarily retired from an active career of performing at concerts, because she felt that her voice was fading. Her only disciple was Smt. Dhondutai Kulkarni, who went on to become a leading vocalist of the Jaipur–Atrauli Gharana, performing for almost eight decades.

In 1977 her voice featured, alongside the likes of Bach, Mozart and Beethoven, on the golden record aboard the NASA spaceship *Voyager*. Kesar Bai's rendition of *'Jaat Kahan Ho'* in *Raag Bhairavi* immortalized a piece of Hindustani classical singing, affirming its position across nations, continents and space till the end of time.

Kesar Bai was known for her reservations regarding recording technologies. Her recording stints between 1935–55 stretched across three brief phases. And one can trace the evolution of her music and style through these records. In 1935, she cut four records for the Madras-based 'Broadcast Record Company', in which she sang the *raags* Gauri, Des, Kafi Kanada, Khambavati, Phag and Bhairavi. These early recordings reflect the influence of the Jaipur–Atrauli *taleem* she received from Alladiya Khan.

During 1945–50, she cut twelve *raags* on six 12-inch records for the HMV label. One can listen to her mature voice in these records, in beautiful *raags* such as Lalit, Malkauns, Paraj, Desi, Kukubh, Bilawal, Jaunpuri, Nand, Durga, Nat Kamod, Lalita, Gauri and Gaud Malhar.

She recorded again for the HMV label between 1953–55 on 10-inch discs. Besides classical *raags*, the nine recordings she did also feature, for the first time, some semi-classical pieces like Hori, Chaiti, Kajri and Bhajans. Due to a dispute between the Gramophone Company and Kesar Bai, these records were released later and never broadcast on the radio. The recordings, as a result, reached very few people. In 1994, however, the Gramophone Company decided to re-issue them on tapes and later on CDs. Kesar Bai's earlier Broadcast label records were also re-issued by Underscore Records Company in 2004. Private collectors who have hours of recordings of Kesar Bai describe her voice as 'The Voice of the Century'.

This page
Above: Bust of Kesar Bai Kerkar by Sarbari Roy Chowdhury

Jaddan Bai

The Progressive

Besides being among the first women to own and run a film studio, Jaddan Bai was perhaps one of the most successful female entrepreneurs of the talkies era in cinema.

Born in Banaras to the famous *tawaif* Daleepa Bai, Jaddan Bai's real-life story is said to have been full of twists and turns. Her early *taleem* began under her parents Daleepa Bai and Miyan Jan, who was a *sarangia* by profession. Her tutelage continued under the *badshah* of Thumri, Ustad Moizuddin Khan, and Barkat Ali Khan, the younger brother of Bade Ghulam Ali Khan. She also took extensive training from Vidwan Dargahiji Misra of Banaras and his son Govardhan Misra, who were eminent *sarangi* players.

As the *tawaif* culture took its last breath amidst all the stigma and a lack of patrons, Jaddan made a bold move and shifted to Bombay, a city where artistes from all over India were converging to become a part of the emerging film industry.

The world of cinema was a dynamic, heterogeneous space, in which Jaddan Bai began negotiating her identity both as a woman and a former *tawaif*. This was a time when the film industry was seeking respectability. Within such an atmosphere of resistance, Jaddan began her short-lived acting career with the movie *Gopichand*, directed by Hakeem Ramprasad of Lahore. However, her achievements as an actress have been overshadowed by her reputation as mother of the legendary Nargis.

In the 1930s, Indian cinema was organized around large film production houses who had their own pool of actors. The robust Jaddan Bai decided to launch her own film company, Sangeet Movietone. In the very first film made under this banner, *Madam Fashion*, Jaddan Bai gave a role to her six-year-old daughter Nargis, whom everyone lovingly called Baby Rani.

Jaddan Bai led the way for women who wanted to find space in the male-dominated world of cinema and its newfound sensibilities. She had great compassion for the lives of professional *tawaifs*, a theme she frequently explored in films made Sangeet Movietone. One of these was the autobiographical *Jeevan Sapna* (1938), in which Jaddan and Dr. Mohan acted; the protagonist was played by the glamorous Mehtab. Nargis's career as an actress too began with woman-centric films like

Darogaji and *Talash-e-Haq*. Jaddan Bai's foray into film production exemplifies the possibilities and the sensitivity of themes that the involvement of women can bring to the silver screen.

At a time of social, cultural and political transition, Jaddan Bai comes across as a woman of great vision and resilience. She often wrote for the newspapers and was also associated with the Progressive Writers Association. Her home was a favourite haunt for artistes, writers, and politicians like Maulana Abdul Kalam Azad, Maulana Shaukat Ali, C.R. Das, Jigar Moradabadi, Josh Malihabadi, Majaz Lucknawi, Sagar Nizami, Hafiz Jullundari and Majrooh Sultanpuri among others. A singer, producer, director, composer and writer, it is difficult even today to find a woman of Jaddan Bai's calibre whose pioneering role in music and cinema paved the way for others to follow.

NARGIS

This page

Above: Film poster of *Hridaymanthan* (1936)
Courtesy: National Film Archive of India, Pune

Left: Actress Nargis
Courtesy: CIViC Archives, New Delhi

Rasoolan Bai

The Voice of Purab Ang

Rasoolan Bai, daughter of Adalat Bai, was born in 1902 in Kachhua Bazaar (Mirzapur) near Banaras. Inheriting the musical legacy of her mother Adalat, Rasoolan displayed a firm grasp over classical *raags* in her childhood. At the age of five, she was sent to learn music under Ustad Shammu Khan of the Ajrara Gharana. Later, she also learnt under the *sarangiyas* (*sarangi* players) Ashiaq Khan and Ustad Maju Khan.

Having mastered genres like Tappa, Purab Ang ki Thumri and Dadra, she ruled the stage for five decades. Often remembered as one of the most illustrious performers of the Banaras Gharana (present-day Varanasi), Rasoolan Bai was particularly known for the power of her voice and the clarity of her rendition. She traversed with ease the Khayal and semi-classical genres like the Thumri.

The decades of her popularity were also the years of nationalist reform movements. The profession of the *tawaif* was no longer recognized for its tradition of *tehzeeb* and cultural refinement. The degenerating institution was abandoned by its patrons and its reputation was maligned by the society. Many women distanced themselves from the *tawaif* community as they found new avenues of singing on gramophone records, and for film and radio. Seeking to escape the stigma, Rasoolan, like many of her contemporaries, is said to have stopped performing the *mujra* in the year 1948. She subsequently moved to the bylanes of Banaras and married a local Banarasi *saree* dealer.

While not more than 15 to 20 of her recordings have survived the travails of time, Rasoolan Bai is still remembered by the music community for her romantic Purab Ang Thumris. She taught her music to Naina Devi, a singer from Calcutta who became a well-known performer herself, gathering accolades particularly for her Thumri renditions. A contemporary of Siddheshwari Devi, Rasoolan Bai often sang for All India Radio and Doordarshan till 1972. However, her life eventually ended in penury, and she was reduced to running a small tea-stall in Allahabad – ironically, right next to the All India Radio building where she once sang.

Rasoolan Bai won the prestigious Sangeet Natak Akademi Award in 1957, becoming the second woman to be honoured with the award, after Kesar Bai Kerkar.

Siddheshwari Devi

Goddess of Thumri

Born in Banaras in 1903 into a family of musicians, Siddheshwari lost both her parents at an early age and was brought up by her aunt, Rajeshwari Devi. Coming from a long line of musicians and singers like Vidyadhari Devi, Rajeshwari Devi and Kamaleshwari Devi, Siddheshwari's fascination with music was natural. Her early inspirations were the records of singers she listened to at her neighbour's place. The first lessons came through observation and imitation. Surprised by her impeccable renditions, Siyaji Maharaj, who came to teach Kamaleshwari, took Siddheshwari under his tutelage.

It was under Siyaji Maharaj, a notable *sarangi* player of Banaras, that Siddheshwari began learning vocals. After his death, she learnt under Rajab Ali Khan of Dewas, a prominent *Khayaliya* of the Jaipur Gharana, and Inayat Khan of Lahore. Much of her later years in training were spent under Bade Ramdas ji, a notable singer of the Banaras Gharana. Siddheshwari gained widespread popularity for her singing, and more particularly for her mastery of the Thumri style. After hearing an intensely emotional rendering of the Bhairavi Thumri ("*Kaahe ko daari re gulal*") by her at an All India Music Conference in Bombay, Ustad Faiyaaz Khan Saheb, the revered exponent of the Agra Gharana, is said to have declared, "After Gauhar, the crown of Thumri rests on your head."

Siddheshwari began receiving invitations from the patron-states of Rampur, Jodhpur, Banaras, Calcutta, Mysore, Lahore and other princely states of the North soon after her first concert in Calcutta at the age of eighteen. Few musicians in recent years have had as vast a repertoire as Siddheshwari Devi. She contributed greatly to the popularity of the Khayal, Thumri, Dadra, Tappa, Kajari, Chaiti and Bhajans. Although she earned accolades as a Thumri singer, her singing reflected intense training in *Khayal Gayaki*.

In 1965, she went on a twelve-day tour to Kabul, performing with the Shah of Kabul who himself was a *sitar* and *sarod* player. Later on in life Siddheshwari Devi joined a music school in Delhi as a professor, and taught there for almost a decade. In recognition of her valuable contribution, she was honoured with the Presidential Award in 1966, the Padma Shri in 1967, a D. Litt. from Rabindra Bharati University and the title of "*Desikottama*" from Visva Bharati University, Santiniketan.

Saraswati Devi

Pioneer of the Talkies

This page
Above: Lobby cards of the films *Jeevan Prabhat* (1937) and *Vachan* (1938)
Courtesy: National Film Archive of India, Pune

Facing page
Film poster of *Achhut Kanya* (1936)
Courtesy: National Film Archive of India, Pune

Saraswati Devi, a distinguished female music director of Hindi cinema, was born in 1912 into a prosperous Parsi family, and was christened Khurshid Minocher Homji. Khurshid had a natural talent and love for music. Her father was a prominent figure of the Parsi community in Bombay. Saraswati's mother was the secretary of the Parsi Gayak Uttejak Mandali (Parsi Music Promotion Society), and it was here that she had her initial training. On V.N. Bhatkhande's advice, she later went to Lucknow's reputed Marris College of Music, known today as Bhatkhande Music University.

Himanshu Rai, an early film director and co-founder of Bombay Talkies, played a major role in Saraswati's entry into the film industry. When Khurshid and her sister Manek first started to work for him as music composer and actor, their decision created an uproar in the Parsi community. This was a time when the film industry as a whole was lobbying for greater respectability and Himanshu Rai was heading this effort. Both sisters had to take on the screen names of Saraswati Devi and Chandraprabha. Saraswati Devi worked for Bombay Talkies from 1934 to 1941. With the setting up of a radio station in Bombay in the late 1920s, she and her sister Manek gave regular musical performances once every month for the programme known as 'Homji Sisters', which became quite popular with the listeners.

Saraswati Devi has several 'firsts' to her credit: she and Jaddan Bai were the first women composers for Indian cinema, and she was amongst the first few music directors to introduce playback singing in Bombay. The first film for which she worked as a music director was *Jawani ki Hawa* (1934), produced by Bombay Talkies. This was a couple of years before playback singing came to dominate films. Many days were spent rehearsing songs with the onscreen duo in this film, Devika Rani and Najmul Husain, before the final recording could take place. Saraswati Devi's first playback assignment came in the year 1936, for the film *Acchut Kanya*. The song '*Kit gaye ho khewan haar*' was supposed to be sung by her younger sister Chandraprabha, who had a sore throat. So Saraswati eventually ended up singing the song from behind the curtain, which also marked the beginning of her elaborate career as playback singer and music director. She was among the first few women who, while dealing with technological limitations, made a considerable contribution to early Indian cinema and to the adaptation of Hindustani music to the new audio-visual medium.

DEVIKA RANI
ACHHUT KANNYA
With
ASHOK KUMAR
अछूत कन्या"
اچھوت کنیا

Akhtari Bai Faizabadi

The Diva of Ghazal

Born in 1914 in Faizabad, at one time the citadel of Awadhi culture, and brought up by a single mother, Mushtari Bai, who was a *tawaif* herself, Akhtari started her career as a performer while still a teenager. During the 1920s, she worked as a stage actress in Calcutta, most often essaying the role of the vamp. In some images from this time she is seen "in a black velvet Western dress and smoking a cigarette with a long black holder". In Lucknow, she set up her own salon, managed very ably by her mother.

Akhtari was by now an artiste of calibre, and only the very distinguished were allowed access to her *mehfils*. She also made a name for herself across North India through a number of 78 rpm recordings released under the Megaphone label. She went on to do a small but successful stint in Hindi films, where she sang and acted as was not uncommon in those days. Even though she was trained by *gharanedaar ustads* in *Khayal Gayaki*, it appeared that she was always attracted to what the purist refers to as 'lighter' genres. This indeed is an irony, given that her greatest contribution to Ghazal singing is the classical treatment she brought to it – the *raagdaari*. She 'lifted' the Ghazal to mainstream music festivals like never before. She also performed the Thumri and Dadra in a unique style quite her own.

Akhtari had a difficult childhood, the poignancy of which pervades her music, stemming perhaps from the experience of loss at an early age. In fact the expression of love as pain is a constant in her work, making the Ghazal an appropriate medium for the expression of her genius. Some of her friends suggest that pain and depression had become such a refrain in her early life that in later years it became a habit – so much so that she liked manufacturing sadness even when there was no reason. Her marriage to the well-known barrister Ishtiaq Ahmed Abbasi brought her closer to Urdu poetry, thanks to his scholarship, but in addition to also the many restrictions of married life. She was eager to win hearts, to be accepted, to feel 'respected'. She became the '*achchi ammi*' of the family, but this also meant altering her intense music career. As women in patriarchal societies, we are familiar with limitations, constraints, and small, confining spaces. Begum Akhtar's situation was compounded by her background of being a *gaanewali*.

Despite these odds she was a woman full of life, humour and zeal. She had innumerable friends, fans and lovers. She was known for her *shaukhi mizaaj*, her humour and wit. Poets of her day wrote specially for her and her singing their work meant a real boost to their careers. Eminent Urdu poets of that time, such as Jigar Moradabadi and Shakeel Badayuni, formed part of Akhtari's inner circle, and she shared close friendships with many like Kaifi Azmi. A free-thinking, fiercely independent woman, she is believed to be the first *vidushi* or *ustani* who stood tradition on its head by tying the *gandaa*, or the official thread that initiates a *shishya* into a learning tradition, on her women students. She was a trend-setter, a diva, even perhaps a rockstar of her times. Hers is the powerful journey of a Bai who became a Begum – Begum Akhtar, as she is remembered by her fans.

KHURSHED
SAFETY MATCHES
MADE IN SWEDEN

SUNDER JAN
SAFETY MATCHES
MADE IN SWEDEN

BAIJEE
WIMCO
SAFETY MATCHES
MADE IN INDIA

MADE IN AUSTRIA
SANICHAR JAN

As proof of their widespread popularity, the *baijis* began to appear in print illustrations on matchbox labels in India and abroad
Courtesy: Parthiv Shah Collection

Photo Courtesy: Parthiv Shah

In Conversation:

Birju Maharaj

Kathak, the North Indian classical dance form, is synonymous with the name of Pandit Birju Maharaj. Born into a family that contributed to Kathak in its present-day form, Maharaj ji is the leading exponent of this form in India and abroad. He started performing and teaching from a very young age, and has taken Kathak to new heights by choreographing dance dramas around the world. A good singer as well, Maharaj ji is a recipient of the Padma Vibhushan, the Sangeet Natak Akademi Award and the Kalidas Samman.

Photo Courtesy: Parthiv Shah

Mujra and the *Tawaif*

The 19th and 20th centuries saw Awadh become the epicentre of North Indian music. Many renowned artistes came from the cities of Lucknow, Banaras and Faizabad. Musical conferences were commonplace in these regions. The Allahabad conference was considered the most famous musical gathering in the North. I grew up in Awadh. My great-grandfathers performed and taught Kathak in the court of Nawab Wajid Ali Shah of Awadh.

I would ask my mother and she would tell me that Babu (Acchan Maharaj, a Kathak Guru and Birju Maharaj's father) has gone to attend a *mujra* in Gorakhpur. I remember this couplet that goes – "Rama sits taking attendance, and gives his people as they deserve"... So *mujra* basically means 'to give attendance'. It is a pure word from Urdu or Farsi, a word of very olden times.

Tawaif, as a word has always carried negative connotations, but in reality *tawaifs* have been students of music, of this rich cultural tradition, like all of us who are learning.

The male dancers had the privilege of performing in the *mandirs*; the *tawaifs* however could perform only at the houses of rich *zamindars* and *nawabs*. Occasions such as the sacred thread ceremony and weddings would feel incomplete without a performance by the *baijis*.

Usually, the *tawaifs* took *taleem* from their Gurus in the morning. Afternoon onwards they would immerse themselves in *shringar* for the evening performance. They were equally adept at singing Khayal as they were at singing Thumri, Dadra and other semi-classical genres. Their performances were followed by *Bhaands* taking the stage, who would then invite the guests to dance along.

For the *baijis*, given the context of their performances, words in songs like *Shyaam*, *Mohan* and *Kanha* were replaced with *yaar* or *balma*, denoting lover.

Most of the Bollywood films you see today portray *tawaifs* in stereotypical ways, with a certain *adaa* of knowing the art of charming men. The *tawaifs* are shown doing *shringar*, or singing and dancing in front of rich *zamindars*, landlords and other patrons. It is true that such performances or *mehfils* did happen, but what is never delved into is the intense *taleem* that these women underwent.

Taleem Khanas

The *Taleem Khanas* were learning centres of dance and music. They were divided into a male space called *mardana* and a female space called *jenana*. Men weren't allowed in the *jenana*. All those who wanted to listen to the *baijis* sing had to stand by the window. The most illustrious of artistes have performed in these *Taleem Khanas* – the list includes the likes of Begum Akhtar, Girija Devi, Rasoolan Bai, Gauhar Jan and Nargis's mother, Jaddan Bai.

My Dada used to teach various facets of performance to the *baijis*. He would especially focus on *abhinaya*, which is an intrinsic part of all performances, be it the Ghazal, Bhajan or Thumri. Dancing and singing are never two separate art forms, you see; *abhinaya* is used everywhere.

In earlier days, *mehfils* were commonplace. They were not hugely pre-planned, but a celebration of our tradition, our togetherness and our love of music. The *mehfil* was a different experience altogether. No concert, no film can match a *mehfil*. Due to the proximity of the dancer and the audience in a *mehfil*, one could explore *bareek bhav* (or, in other words, fine gestures) – which can never be visible in an auditorium. I tried teaching Madhuri Dixit *bareek bhav* for the film *Devdas*. One of the advantages of the camera in films these days is that it can zoom in to get the most intricate of details, the finest of gestures, which stage performers cannot expect people in an auditorium to see.

This was the general ambience of Lucknow, music flowing everywhere – in temples, village *chaurahas*, *chabootaras* and *aangans*.

The Gramophone

I have heard gramophone recordings but the magic of a live performance can never be matched. One cannot see the artist's expressions, nor their *abhinaya*. These days, in the video, one can not only hear but also see the artiste performing, but still, the essence of performance is only when there is a live audience. Ours is not merely an audio or visual art form but a performative culture, which finds a new life each time it is performed in front of a live audience.

When I would sing on the radio, I would think, "What is it that I sing for into the microphone?" I need faces, I need eyes to match, and feedback. Without getting a response from my listeners, without hearing *waah-waahs*, how do you expect an artiste to perform? We are used to instantaneous feedback from people.

Photos courtesy: Birju Maharaj

JALSAGHAR

The Singing Space

Photographs by Parthiv Shah

Music and dance for entertainment, celebration and on religious occasions were very important facets of the lives of the elite, particularly the landed gentry or zamindars. Their forms and lyrics were fashioned after the varying modalities of different occasions: familial ceremonies, religious celebrations, seasonal ensembles, daily rituals, marriages, festivals and so on. These performances held in *havelis* and *jalsaghars* were leisurely affairs, and were closely connected to defined physical spaces. For instance, the word *haveli* in Haveli Sangeet, a form of devotional singing, defined a 'home' for Krishna, and the songs themselves were a medium for the Pushtimargi Vaishnava (devotees of Krishna who follow the path of grace) devotees to worship.

Before music was inscribed on wax and lacquer to be made available for general audience, it was in the *jalsaghars* that the lives of the *baijis* unfolded. It was here that their performances took place, poetry was read, and music staged without the present day's electronic embellishments. But their intriguing life stories, their distinct lifestyles and the order of their performances rest largely or anecdotes, and are often shrouded in mystery and denial.

Over the years, these places of performance, *jalsaghars* as they were popularly known, have lost their audience, the lively retinues of singers and accompanists, and the traditions that upheld their existence. Now all that remains are the ruins of an old-worldly charm. This series of photographs captures the remains of the theatrical ambience that the *jalsaghars* were witness to. The visual journey invokes their antiquity inscribed in the present, and the nostalgia of the musical traditions that have over the years decorated the architecture of these glorious buildings.

Travelling through the *baris*, the life of the artefacts caught in the camera lens tends to recreate these experiences from a time long gone and now forgotten, but that still somehow breathes through the ageing curios – the portraits of patrons and singers, the quiet *baithak*, the cold chandeliers, the colonial split windows, the waiting balconies...

PATHURIAGHATA

Ghosh Bari

The Ghosh Bari at Pathuriaghata has been the cynosure of musical gatherings since colonial times. A witness to performances by the likes of Gauhar Jan and Kesar Bai, this relic from the past is currently maintained by the Ghose family.

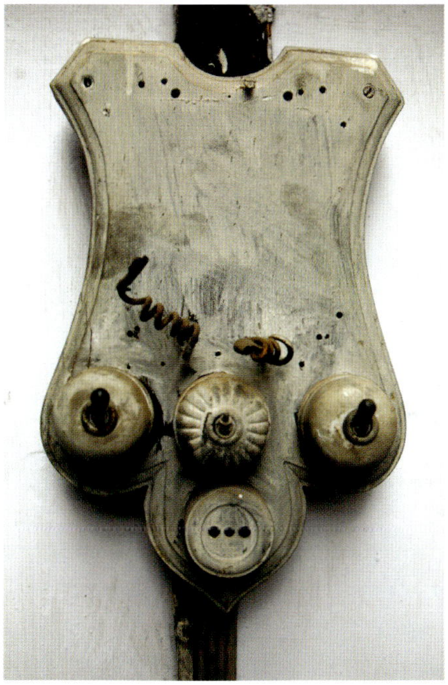

BEHALA

Roy Bari

Famous for its Puja celebrations, a tradition started by Ambika Charan Roy in 1756, this *bari* was once known for its musical assemblies among the nobility.

SHOVABAZAR

Raj Bari

Built in the 18th century by Raja Nabakrishna Deb, this royal building is known for the widescale Durga Puja celebrations begun in 1757 by the king himself and performed every year since then. Maintained now by the Deb family, this palace in ruins has held numerous *jalsas* over two centuries.

MANUFACTURED BY
RECORD MFG.
HINDUSTHAN
RECORDS
मेगाफोन
TRADE MARK
Megaphone

GRAMOPHONE, BAIJIS AND THE

National Movement

The Indian independence movement, perhaps for the first time, brought out the subversive potential of the gramophone. A technology that originated in the west was now co-opted by Indians to voice their protest against foreign occupation and the monopoly enjoyed by foreign companies. On the other hand, the wealth that the singers had generated through professional singing now funded the freedom struggle.

Swadeshi Records, a label founded by H. Bose, was among the first to record Gurudev Rabindranath Tagore. However, the batch of cylinder records inscribed with songs for the Swadeshi Movement never really made it into the market as the records were seized by the police under the British administration. It is believed that H. Bose later sent Tagore's recording of *Vande Mataram* to France for disc pressing.

Throughout India, many native labels were floated by Indians who had earlier held dealerships of foreign companies. The many versions of *Vande Mataram* recorded by Indian companies during the national movement serve as an example of the nationalist sensibility that pervaded the entire music industry.

In 1935, a businessman from Ahmedabad by the name of Dulerai Pandya found considerable financial backing to form The National Gramophone Record Manufacturing Co. Ltd., with offices in Bombay and a factory at Wadala in the northern suburbs of the city with technical support from Japan. Pandit Jawaharlal Nehru, whose "Message to the Countrymen" was recorded, inaugurated the factory. The records displayed the tricolour flag and the brand name 'Young India' was chosen to appeal to the nation's youth. The rise of The National Gramophone Record Manufacturing Co. Ltd. and its label, Young India, was the most serious attempt to break the monopoly that The Gramophone Company Ltd. had held for several decades. The company not only signed the Prabhat film company on a contract, but also engaged a number of 'private recorders' – as had The Gramophone Company Ltd. – to extend its market share of products.

The women singers had a more difficult path to tread. They performed generously for charity to collect party funds and their dwelling places often served as shelter for Indian revolutionaries in hiding. Despite their efforts to contribute to the national movement, however, their presence was disregarded and even condemned because of the societal stigma attached to their profession.

Various Indian labels came up in different parts of the country emulating the spirit of *swadeshi*: Vielophone, Ramagraph, Megaphone, Binapani, New Theatre Records, Kohinoor Records, Senola Records, Hindustan Records, Maxitone Records.

The national movement was not only a struggle against foreign rule, but it had a social reform agenda as well. Having dealt with opposition from the colonial authorities, the *tawaifs* found that they now had to face strident attacks from the reformers in their own society. The reform movement and changing patronage had an adverse influence both on their art and their lives. Their struggles now constituted exploring new, respectable platforms for performance, coping with the changing socio-economic and musical scenarios, and resisting the colonial rule while striving for survival.

Yet many of the *baijis* are remembered to this day for not only warding off the stigmas forced upon them by a conservative society, but also for deploying the wealth and influence they garnered from their recording careers in the upliftment of singing communities and support for female artistes. Anjani Bai Malpekar, a doyen of the Bhendi Bazaar Gharana, was known to have worked fervently to improve the status of Kalawants, the community of Goan singing women that she herself came from. She was particularly instrumental in abolishing the custom of wearing *pesvad* during performances, to distinguish respectable women from dancers and singers. The association also protested against the allocation of separate housing for the community of Kalawants. Kananbala, a famous Bengali singer and actor who later turned producer, laid the foundations of Mahila Shilpi Mahal to support struggling female artistes in the Bengali film industry. The left-leaning Progressive Writers Association (PWA) was financially supported by Jaddan Bai, mother of actress Nargis and founder of the film company Sangeet Movietone. Imam Bandi of Lahore fearlessly provided shelter to freedom fighters during police raids.

However, this was also a time in India's history when the nationalist discourse and the subsequent moral standards led to a drastic reconstruction of traditional centres of culture. The musical and dancing arts were not left untouched by the larger movements of reform pervading Indian society. The idea perhaps was to lose the baggage of colonial degeneration in order to restore India to the glory of the pre-colonial era. The marginalization of *baijis* was perhaps inevitable in the face of a cultural restoration that failed to recognize the complex domain of traditional performers. Eventually pushed out of their established roles, the *baijis* endeavoured to redeem their art through film and radio, the popular cultural mediums of new India. This is not to say that their entry was unanimously welcomed, but amidst all the criticism and opposition they also found people who valued their artistry and facilitated the transition that had become a necessity.

This page
Above: Film poster of *Vidyapati* (1937)
Courtesy: National Film Archive of India, Pune

Left: A magazine advertisement for an Indian record company
Courtesy: SIRC, Mumbai

MUSICAL
Rivalries

Unlike the cinema and radio, gramophone recordings began as a private enterprise and remained so. Emile Berliner's The Gramophone Company, which later came to be known as Gramophone and Typewriters Limited (GTL), was among the first few enterprises in the world to explore offshore markets. GTL, which launched the recording label HMV, was undoubtedly one of the most successful companies with operations in India. However, many native enterprises in collaboration with foreign companies were floated around the same time, given the popularity of records and their widespread demand.

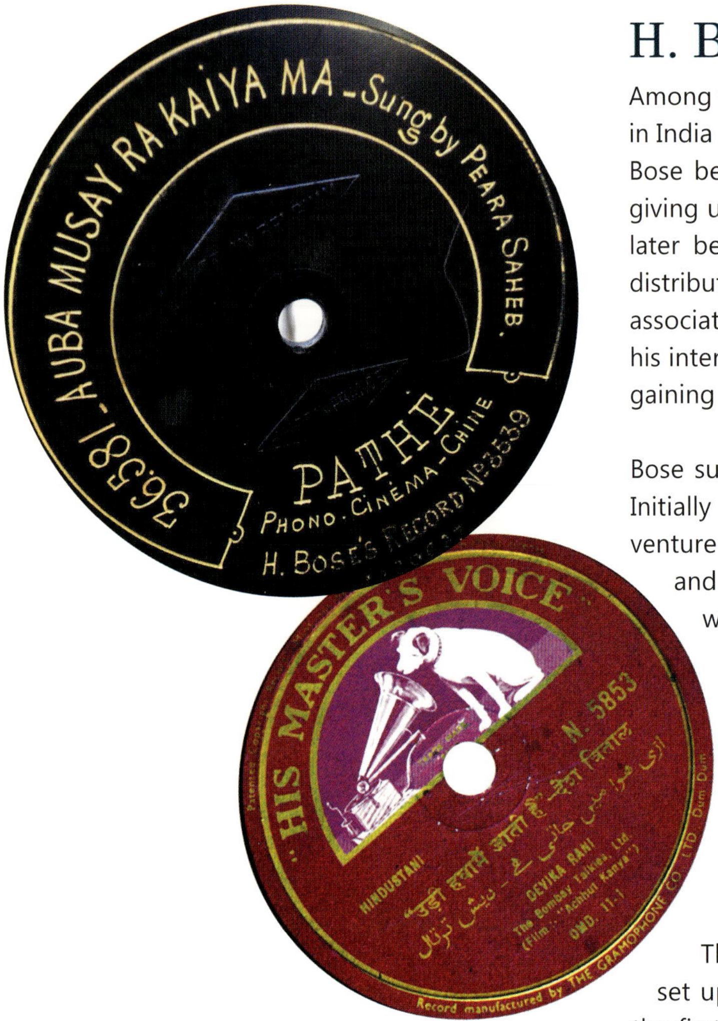

H. Bose's Swadeshi Records

Among the first entrepreneurs to venture into gramophone recording in India was H. Bose of H. Bose and Co., Calcutta. A remarkable figure, Bose began a business in perfume and toiletries in the 1900s after giving up a career in medicine. He soon opened a printing press and later became the proud owner of an indigenous cycle works and distributor of 'Rover' cycles in 1903. In the same year Bose formed an association with the local agents of Pathe Feres in Paris because of his interest in cinema, a medium that was still in its infancy but slowly gaining popularity.

Bose successfully began marketing the Pathe phonographs in 1904. Initially operating from his cycle stores, the profits from the new venture helped him to open an exclusive showroom for phonographs and cylindrical records at Marble House, Calcutta. The showroom was called the 'The Talking Machine Hall'.

Bose's association with Pathe precipitated the making of a series of cylindrical records with Bengali artistes. Interestingly, he was able to bring several respected names, including Rabindranath Tagore, Lal Chandra Boral and Kashinath Chatterjee of Star Theatres, to record for him in accordance with the *swadeshi* spirit.

These records became so popular that H. Bose decided to set up his own manufacturing unit for cylindrical records in 1907, the first of its kind in India. Bose's company, Swadeshi Records, had the largest network of recording agents covering a majority of the Eastern Provinces and North Indian states. The political appeal of the indigenous enterprise was obvious in the company's full-page newspaper advertisements:

"Mr. H. Bose is the first to manufacture records here in Calcutta and his are now the only real Swadeshi Records. Even the blanks are manufactured here – and the songs which are recorded today are offered to the public the day after. The manufacture of these records marks an important epoch in the industrial enterprise of India. It points out most clearly that the Indians, if they care to turn their attention, not only compete fairly with other nations, but in some cases beat them."

By 1908, around 500 titles were released on cylinders under Bose's label. However, recording discs had gained significant popularity over cylinders by that time. Enterprising as always, Bose decided to re-release the recordings on 'discs' under Pathe, to capitalize on the growing popularity of the new medium and local music.

The production of cylinders came to a halt, but Bose continued to arrange recordings with local artistes for Pathe in India, which had by then extended its operations as far as Ceylon and Burma.

Bose's rapport with regional artistes and his entrepreneurial spirit brought together a community of singers, paving the way for the popularity of the medium and the fertile beginnings of sound recording in India.

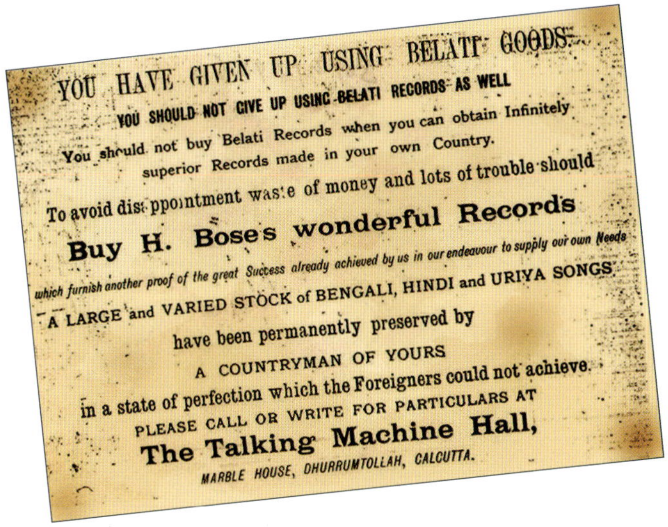

Valabhdas Runchordas's The Talking Machine and Indian Records Co.

In the year 1902, Valabhdas Runchordas, a businessman from Ahmedabad, founded Valabhdas Lakhmidas and Co. in Bombay, in partnership with Lakhmidas Rowjee Tairsee. The firm, which initially dealt in medicine, toiletries, snacks and hardware, was soon to become one of the largest resellers and distributors of talking machines in the Indian subcontinent, under a sub-venture called The Talking Machine and Indian Records Co.

Valabhdas's company already had the dealership for the machines and records of Edison Phonographs, Columbia Records and Pathe in Bombay, before a German company by the name of Beka entered the Indian market.

Beka, a record company operating from Berlin, began its Far Eastern expeditions in the year 1905. Valabhdas Lakhmidas and Co. not only helped arrange local artistes for Beka's recordings in Bombay, but also facilitated the recording of several North Indian artistes. With their help, Beka's engineers were able to conduct over 300 recordings in Bombay and Calcutta, before departing to Germany for processing the records.

In 1906, Valabhdas Lakhmidas and Co. opened a sub-division called The Talking Machine and Indian Records Co., to handle the distribution for Beka's recordings. Within a year, this company became the sole agents of Beka's Indian repertory, as well as their distributors in Burma and Ceylon.

The Talking Machine and Indian Records Co. continued to facilitate Beka's recording expeditions and distribution in India till it launched its own line of gramophones called the VIEL-O-PHONE. These machines were manufactured in Germany by Carl Lindstrom A.G., which absorbed companies like Beka, Odeon and The International Talking Machine Co. in later years.

This page
Above: An H Bose advertisement, urging Indians to buy Indian Record labels
Courtesy: Vibodh Parthasarthi

Below: Singer Lal Chandra Boral

Surendra Nath Mukharji's Royal Record

Surendra Nath Mukharji's company Mukherjee and Mukharji dealt in electrical and mechanical products before bagging a dealership with the French company Nicole Records in 1904.

Mukharjee and Mukharji continued its operations for Nicole Records and simultaneously took on dealerships of other foreign labels in India. The company's bold move came with the introduction of indigenously produced disc records of local music in 1906. Mukharji's own make of disc records was marketed under the label Royal Record, and the initial recordings sold were by famed singers like Gauhar Jan of Calcutta. These were the first 'flat disc single sided records' produced in India.

However, the label is said to have been discontinued later when faced with fierce competition from western companies who had the advantage of huge financial and technological resources.

Ramchunder Narrotumdas's RAM-A-PHONE Disc Record

The Narrotumdas family run T.S. Ramchunder and Bros. originally dealt in the manufacture of musical instruments. Founded in Bombay, the company's first encounter with sound recording was through a dealership of Edison Phonographs in India in the early 1900s.

The indigenous firm soon entered into an association with Lyrophone Werke to produce its own line of records under the label RAM-A-PHONE. The first recordings were conducted by engineers of Lyrophone in 1906, and were released a year later in 1907. The name of the label was later changed to RAMAGRAPH.

While RAMAGRAPH was one of the largest selling indigenously produced labels, the discs used by it were never manufactured in India. The discs were pressed in Germany and supplied by Lyrophone and later by Carl Lindstorm A.G.

RAMAGRAPH remained the one of the most popular Indian labels till it ceased production in the 1930s.

••••••••••••••••••

James Opera Record of James Manufacturing Co., Bombay, founded by Hormusjee N. Mehta and Jeevanjee D. Mehta, and Singer Record,

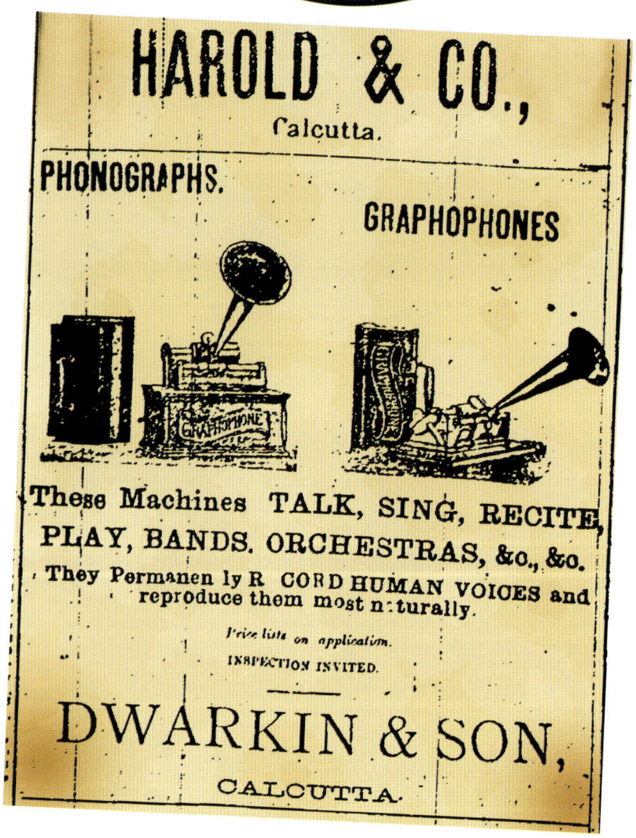

This page
Above: A gramophone advertisement for a native distributer in Calcutta
Courtesy: Vibodh Parthasarathi

established by Rustom B. Lala and Nanabhoy J. Mody, were other important Indian labels released in the 1900s. While many native businessmen tried to establish indigenous labels, the two who came closest to running successful companies were Surendra Nath Mukharji and H. Bose. Both Mukharji and Bose appealed to the '*swadeshi*' sentiments of the Indian people by selling records 'that were made in India'. It was hardly a coincidence that many Indian record labels released *Vande Mataram*, a song of patriotic fervour, to show their association with the cause of India's freedom.

On the other hand, the advertisements for foreign labels attempted to 'Indianize' this western invention by associating it with mythological figures and religious rituals. One of the famous advertisements featured an image of the Hindu goddess Saraswati with a gramophone on her lap.

The enormous market in India and the large supplies of shellac induced many rival companies from England, France and Germany to make their way to India. Between 1902 and 1916, over 70 different labels, both native and foreign, were selling music to Indian audiences; the important ones were Beka, Universal, Columbia, HMV, RAMAGRAPH, Nicole, Elephone, Odeon, Pathe, Neophone, H. Bose, Kamla, Binapani, Royal, James Opera, Singer and Sun.

The enthusiasm that marked the entry of this musical novelty in India began to fade in the 1950s as it lost its audience to film, radio and later, television. Still, admirers of old-world charm and musical purists prefer their vinyls to vast repositories of digital music.

This page
Left: A gramophone advertisement featuring the Hindu goddess Saraswati

FROM THEATRE TO Cinema

Theatre was amongst the most popular mediums of entertainment in the pre-gramophone era. More so than the performances of courtesans because of its socio-mythological themes and its easier access by the general population. Theatre nevertheless did share some of the stigma of the so-called vulgar arts, and for a long time female roles were essayed by men.

One reason for the theatre's popularity was its commitment to the local idiom. In one sense regional drama companies were precursors to later forms of entertainment like the gramophone, film and radio, often acting as repositories of themes and talent. Many theatre company owners conducted novel experiments with the new mediums of cinema and recording.

Drama companies were among the first places to be frequented by recording agents to recruit singing talent. In 1902, GTL's first recording in Calcutta was facilitated by Amarendra Nath Dutta, owner of Classic Theatre. The singers were two teen artistes, Miss Soshi Mukhi and Fani Bala, who were part of Dutta's drama company. Considering the popularity of the medium, the drama companies soon started to put out dialogues, songs and orchestral pieces from popular plays.

Some of the best singers and actors of the early talkie era in films began their careers with regional theatre companies. Angurbala, the famous Nazrul singer, started out as a singer–actor with Bengali theatre companies like Star Theatre and Cornwallis, before she landed film roles alongside the likes of Indubala and Kamala Jharia. In Maharashtra, Bai Sundara Bai was known for her contribution to Lavani, a form of Marathi dance-theatre, and she even composed music for theatrical productions that included singers of such repute as Bal Gandharva. She later went on to work with the visionary film director, V. Shantaram.

In the early decades of the Indian talkie, the recording of songs was an arduous task. The musical accompanists had to be kept beyond the view of the camera, or hiding behind the property on the sets. The protagonists of the film had to sing while acting with certain movements. For filming a song of three minutes, several rehearsals were required and many songs were presented with close-up shots of the actors. The main obstacle was that most actors were poor singers. It was a difficult job to train them to sing in tune with the accompanists. The stage actors who were used to longer renditions had to be trained to reduce their singing to just over three minutes due to the technological limitation of the 78 rpm record. So, singing in films was an ordeal for many.

The music director of Bombay Talkies, Saraswati Devi, one of the first female composers in the film industry (1912–1980), made a lot of effort to train artistes like Devika Rani and Ashok Kumar. The technological limitations of early cinema created a demand for the singer–actor, a role for which *baijis* were perhaps the most competent. However, the transition of female recording artistes to talkies cannot be attributed to a single cause.

This page
Angurbala

Facing page
Film poster of *Bhabhi* (1938), music director: Saraswati Devi
Courtesy: National Film Archive of India, Pune

'Performance' was not the only thing common between the world of *baijis* and the world of cinema. Despite the popularity of cinema,

A BOMBAY TALKIES PICTURE
CO-STARRING
RENUKA DEVI
AND
R. JAIRAJ
WITH
MEERA
AND
MAYA DEVI
'BHABI'
ਭਾਬੀ
بھابی
Chandawarkar

"कुंकू"
"The UNEXPECTED"
प्रभात चित्र

filmmakers struggled to find willing actors because working in films was considered a taboo. The Father of Indian Cinema, Dada Saheb Phalke, the director who made India's first talkie, *Raja Harishchandra*, has recalled in his memoir how he managed to cast a woman from a salon for the role of Taramati, Harishchandra's wife. The female actor left, however, before Phalke could complete the film. He eventually had to cast Anna Salunke, a cook in a restaurant he frequented, as Taramati. Salunke went on to play many female leads in Phalke's productions.

The taboo eventually wore off as the medium gained even more popularity and public acceptance. Still, for a long time, women from respectable families kept their distance. This is apparent from the long list of female actors in Indian cinema who were either Anglo-Indians, stage artistes or singer–dancers. Not to mention that the arts of singing and dancing, and theatre as well, fell into the category of vulgar professions.

For the *baijis* who had dominated the recording industry, talkies seemed to be the natural way ahead. These women not only gave Indian cinema some of its most memorable roles in the early years, but also, challenging the conventions of the time, made successful writers, directors and producers. Long before playback singing brought relief to talkie actors, women like Ishrat Sultana (a.k.a. Bibbo) and Jahan Ara Kajjan (a.k.a. Kajjan Bai) acted, sang and composed music for major hits produced by prominent film companied like Sagar Movietone, Madan Theatres, Calcutta's New Theatres, Ajanta Movietone and many

Facing page
Film poster of *Kunku* (1937), actress: Shanta Apte
Courtesy: National Film Archive of India, Pune

This page
Clockwise, from above left: Lobby card of film *Azad* (1940), music director: Saraswati Devi
Courtesy: National Film Archive of India, Pune
Indubala, Jahan Ara Kajjan

लक्ष्मी प्रोडक्शन्स· प्रणीत
का द म्ब री
LAXMI
PRODUCTIONS
Laxmi Productions'
PROUD PRESENTATION
KADAMBARI
SHANTA APTE VANMALA
PAHARI SANYAL
HARISH JIVAN JAGDISH
Director
NANDLAL JASWANTLAL
A SUPREME RELEASE

others. Ishrat, the daughter of a Delhi courtesan Hafeeza Jan, began her career as a singer for India's first talkie, *Alam Ara*. She received her first professional credit for Ajanta Movietone's *Rangila Rajput* (1933). Kajjan Bai's first role came with Madan Theatre's *Shirin Farad* (1931). She however gained numerous accolades for her work in *Indra Sabha*. Produced by Madan Theatres merely a year after India's first talkie, this musical with 71 songs had a run time of 211 minutes, and still holds the world record for the film with the most number of songs.

As live singing gave way to playback in the 1930s, names like Amir Bai Karnataki, Nalini Jaiwant, Leela Chitnis, Devikarani, Snehprabha Pradhan, Shamshad Begum, Nurjahan, Suraiya, Zohra Bai Ambalewali, Indubala, Angurbala and Kamla Jharia cemented the foundations of Hindustani music in Indian cinema. Breaking the usual ranks of a male-dominated industry, women like Saraswati Devi made a name by composing music for visionary directors like Himanshu Rai. Others like Jaddan Bai and Kanan Devi went on to found their own production houses, contributing to women-centric cinema and supporting fellow female artistes.

By the 1950s, the recording industry was in decline as film and radio gained widespread popularity. The rise of cinema coincided with the fall of the courtesan culture in the wake of reform movements. The transition from gramophone to film and radio was obviously a matter of survival. But, breaking stereotypes and taboos, their illustrious careers were not mere miracles of destiny. Years of hard work went into trying to adapt to newfound roles and technologies in a male-dominated industry. Many must have failed, but those who managed to survive and succeed wrote an unforgettable chapter of Indian history.

Facing page
Film poster of *Kadambari* (1944)
Courtesy: National Film Archive of India, Pune

This page:
Above: Still from the film *Nirmala* (1938)
Courtesy: National Film Archive of India, Pune

This page
Actress Husn Bano
Courtesy: CIViC Archive, New Delhi

Facing page
Clockwise, from top left:
Actresses Swarnalata, Chandraprabha, Shobhana Samarth, Suraiya
Courtesy: CIViC Archive, New Delhi

स्वर्णलता—जस्टिस में

★ चन्द्रप्रभा सामाजिक चित्र

सुरैया

शोभना समर्थ

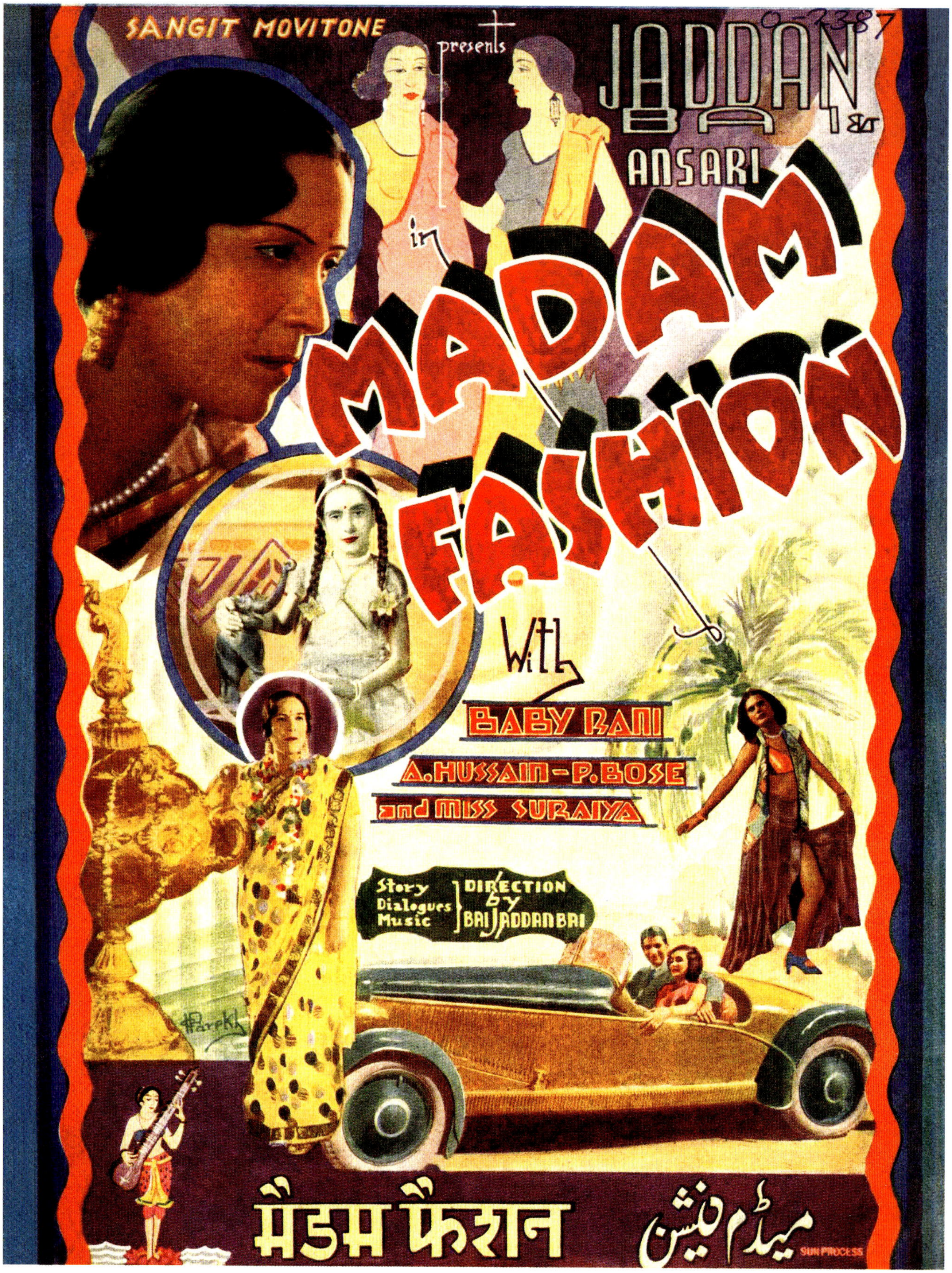
SANGIT MOVITONE
presents
JADDAN BAI
ANSARI
in
MADAM FASHION
With
BABY RANI
A.HUSSAIN-P.BOSE
and MISS SURAIYA
Story
Dialogues
Music
DIRECTION by BAI JADDANBAI
मैडम फैशन
میڈم فیشن
SUN PROCESS

MADAM FASHION

CAST OF CHARACTERS

JUGALKISHORE	A. HUSEIN
AMARNATH	ANSARI
JAGDEESHKUMAR	P. BOSE
NIRANJAN PRASHAD	MISRA
TARACHAND	YUSUF
RAMOO	M. P. SINHA
SHEELADEVI	BAI JADDANBAI
BABY	BABY RANI
LEELEE	Miss SURAYYA
LAXMI	NAJNEEN BEGUM
ROJ	Mrs. NANJAPPA

Sound Recording: M. I. Dharamsey.

Photography: Jagatbhanoo *and* Rajanikant Pandye.

Direction: BAI JADDANBAI.

Story, Dialogues and Music Direction: BAI JADDANBAI.

भारत की सुप्रसिद्ध संगीत फिल्म कम्पनी का सर्वांग सुन्दर हाहाकारमय तथा हास्यरस से परीपूर्ण अनोखा सामाजीक चीत्रपट.

★ मैडम फ़ैशन ★

मैडम फ़ैशन में पात्रों तथा अभिनेताओं की नामावली:—

जुगल किशोर	ए. हुसैन
अमरनाथ	अन्सारी
जगदीश कुमार	पी. बोस
निरंजन प्रशाद	मिसरा
ताराचन्द	यूसुफ़
रामू	एम. पी. सिन्हा
शीलादेवी	बाई जद्दन बाई
बेबी	बेबी रानी
लीली	मिस सुरैया
लक्ष्मी	नाज़नीन बेगम
रोज	मिसीज़ नानजप्पा

डायरेक्शन:—बाई जद्दन बाई.

कहानी, संवाद तथा गायन दिग्दर्शक:—बाई जद्दन बाई.

ध्वनीआलेखक:—एम. आई. धर्मसी.

चित्रालेखक:—जगत भानू तथा रजनी कान्त पान्डेय.

—:बाई जद्दन बाई की अपूर्व भेंट:—

— મેડમ ફેશનના ગાયનો —

શીલા— ૧

રાગ—ગંધારી.

છુમ છનાનનનન બિછવા બાજે.

બેબી— ૨

કબસી હૈ પ્યારી—યેહ ગુળયા હમારી
મેં જાઉં બલહારી.
અપની સખીયોંકો બુલાઉં ધૂમસે બ્યાહ રચાઉં,
લાઉંગી સારી—ઔર ગોટા કિનારી
મેં જાઉં બલહારી.

શીલા—

તુ મુજકો જાનસે પ્યારી હૈ ઓ મેરી ગુળયા,
યેહ પ્યારી ગુળયા તેરી ઔર તુ મેરી ગુળયા.
તુ ખેલ સાથમેં ઇસકે મેં તુજસે ખેલુંગી.
તુ ઇસકા પ્યાર લે મેં તેરા પ્યાર લેલુંગી,
બેબી હમારી મેં જાઉં બલહારી—તુ હૈ મેરી પ્યારી.

શીલા— ૩

હો પ્યાલા મધકા ભરા હુવા,
જાયે રાત સોલા સીંગાર હો
હો કહીં સીતારે ચમક રહે.
કહીં ચંદ્રમાં કી બહાર હો.
હો કહીં પે કોયલ કુકતી,
તો કહીં પે મોર હો નાચતા.
ઔર કહીં પપીહાકી હો સદા,
કહીં બુલબુલોં કી પુકાર હો.
કોઇ હો કીસી કો ગલે લગાએ
કોઈ રૂઠ જાયે કોઈ મનાએ.
ઔર હસે કોઈ કોઈ મુસકુરાયે
કહીં પ્રેમ હો કહીં પ્યાર હો—

જુગલ— ૪

પ્રેમહી દરયા પ્રેમહી નય્યા પ્રેમહી ખેવન હાર,
પ્રેમ ભંવર ઔર પ્રેમ કિનારા પ્રેમ પે કુલ આધાર.
પ્રેમહી મંદીર પ્રેમ પુજારી પ્રેમ ગુંધાએ હાર,
પ્રેમહી દેવી પ્રેમહી દેવતા પ્રેમ કે કુલ અવતાર.
પ્રેમહી દર્પન પ્રેમહી દર્શન પ્રેમ જગત સીંગાર,
પ્રેમ બનાએ પ્રેમ બિગાડે પ્રેમહી જગકા સાર.
પ્રેમમેં જીના પ્રેમમે મરના, પ્રેમ જીવન આધાર.
પ્રેમ જીવનકા સચ્ચા સાથી, પ્રેમસે બેડા પાર.

૫

ચલી જા મોરી નૈયા કિનારે કિનારે
ગહરી નદિયા દુર કિનારા
ખેવન વાલે મનવારે—ચલીજા—

શીલા— ૬

પીકે હમ તુમ જો ચલે ઝુમતે મૈ ખાનેસે,
ઝુક કે કુચ્છ બાત કરી શીશેને પય માનેસે.
તુજકો ક્યા ફાયદા હૈ બગુમમે જલ જાનેસે,
શમઅને યહ ભી ન પુછા કભી પરવાનેસે.
આપ આજાએ તો શાયદ કે કરાર આ જાએ,
દીલે બેતાબ બહેલતા નહિ બહેલાનેસે.
હમને દેખી હૈ કીસી શોખકી મસ્તી ભરી આંખ,
મીલતી જુલતી હય છલકતે હુવે પયમાને સે.

શીલા— ૭

કબસી યેહ ધુમ મચાઈ કનૈયા ગારી મેં દુંગી.
ભર પીચકારી મુખપર મારી
ભીજ ગઇ તન સારી.
ખેલન આયે હો નાર પરાઇ સે
કબસી યેહ હૈ નીઠરાઈ.

Our Next

TRANSPORTATION FOR LIFE

◆

(REGISTERED)

◆

Featuring:

SANGEFT GALAXY OF STARS

◆

For Booking Apply to:—

SANGEET MOVIETONE Co.,

24, Babulnath Road, ... BOMBAY. 7.

Printed at New Jack Printing Works.

Facing page
Film poster of *Madam Fashion* (1936)
Courtesy: National Film Archive of India, Pune

This page
Excerpts from a booklet of the film *Madam Fashion*
Courtesy: National Film Archive of India, Pune

Photo courtesy: Parthiv Shah

In Conversation:

Shyam Benegal

Director and screen writer Shyam Benegal changed the way films were conceptualized in India with his version of Alternative Cinema in the 1970s. He has seven National Film Awards to his credit for best Hindi features. He has been appointed Chairman to the prestigious Film and Television Institute of India (FTII) twice while also teaching there. A recipient of the Dada Saheb Phalke Award in 2005, and a Padma Shri and Padma Bhushan awardee, Benegal is also noted for his keen interest in Hindustani music, which inspired films like *Mandi* and *Sardari Begum*.

The Gramophone as a Catalyst of Change

The Indian music scenario changed drastically with the introduction of the gramophone. I think Gauhar Jan's career perfectly illustrates how things changed with the onset of such recording technology. A dancer and singer from Calcutta, she was one of the first to record on a gramophone. In her case, the gramophone comes across as a central image of transition: a transition between generations, from old to new; a transition from singing courtesan, a *kothewali*, to a professional recording artiste. She became the bridge between the past of the *kothas* of Lucknow, Uttar Pradesh and Delhi, and the future of professional recording artistes. And the catalyst of this change was the gramophone.

This was an age when people were scared of singing into microphones and losing their voices. So one can understand why singing on the gramophone did not come naturally to Indian vocalists. For instance, to convince Gauhar Jan for her first recording, the recording agent brought some of his own music to play. By the end of the recording she was really upset, because this was probably the first time she was timed to sing an entire *raag* in three minutes.

When one goes for a *baithak* or a concert, the whole atmosphere is one that is geared for a performance, where the artistic expression is not curbed by the exigencies of time. The singer explores the various strands of the *raag* through the evening, through the night – so the expositions would be much more leisurely. Not only leisurely, but it would allow the singer to go into patterns that were far more intricate – an elaborate design of melodies. But once we start to limit them to time, obviously, it is bound to have its effect on the style. And that is exactly what the gramophone did.

In all of this change there were also those who managed this transition brilliantly. Great singers like Faiyaz – they managed to do that excellently for the gramophone. Presenting a Khayal concisely in 3–5 minutes was a massive shift in the way a Khayal had been sung before. Artistes like Faiyaz Khan, Bade Ghulam Ali Khan and Heera Bai's father – Abdul Karim Khan – adapted wonderfully.

Abdul Karim Khan was an absolute master and he did any number of *raags* in three to three-and-a-half minutes, including announcing his own name and ending with it. As they say, he was in fact born for the microphone; his records are what made North Indian classical music popular with the people.

Changing Spaces for Performance

Looking at history, one finds there are so many things that are at work – we talk about an art form, the evolution of art forms of different kinds, and the vehicle that takes these art forms to the audiences. For instance, with the decline of the courts, a shift in patronage meant that music had to find its way to the audience in a different way.

In the time of Bahadur Shah Zafar, the repository rested with the court musicians in Delhi, and the same goes for Lucknow and other smaller places in Uttar Pradesh and Bihar. But gradually, when these centres started to crumble, music had to find newer platforms. Interestingly, one of the most important places where these traditions found shelter was the *kotha*.

Great singers like Faiyaz Khan and Bade Gulam Ali Khan belonged to the era when major shifts were taking place. This music culture was concentrated in one region because of the courts. When the patronage changed from the aristocracy to traders, one can see a clear shift: to places like Bombay and to some extent Calcutta, where the mill owners were now the new patrons. I personally think that Bombay became a new centre, whether you think of Heera Bai or Kesar Bai or the whole bunch of singers from that time.

> “Nobody thought of Shanta Apte, the great singer-actress of Hindi and Marathi cinema, as a celebrity, like Aishwarya Rai today, or someone you would like to meet and get an autograph from. On the contrary, in those times, people would try to hide any encounter or association with the actresses.”

When Mogubai Refused to Sing...

Getting classical musicians to give their voices for the talkies was never easy. Especially, the older generation of singers felt that these newer technologies were not dignified enough for their art.

When I was making *Bhumika*, I planned to convince Mogubai to lend her voice for the grandmother's character, and Mogubai's daughter, the famous Kishori Amonkar, to sing for the daughter's character.

Mogubai lived between my office and home, and I passed her house every day on my way to the office and back. When I approached Kishori with the idea, she was very enthusiastic about the project. But when I asked if she thought her mother would agree to sing, Kishori promptly replied, "Don't be surprised if she throws you out of the house."

Nonetheless I took my chances, and asked Kishori to accompany me. At Mogubai's place, as we started to talk, she asked me:
"What do you want me to sing for?"
I explained, "A film."
"For a film?" She pointed to the huge portrait hanging above us.
"Do you know who that is?"

This page:
Mogubai Kurdikar

This page:
Above: Film poster of *Zubeidaa* (2001)
Below: Film poster of *Sardari Begum* (1996)

Facing page:
Film poster of *Bhumika* (1977)

"Yes, he is Ustad Alladiya Khan", I said.
Mogubai looked up again and said, "No, he is God."

I think she felt insulted because I had simply called him "Ustad". This was the level of devotion students had for their Gurus.

Mogubai eventually told me she wasn't a Bai who sings songs on which some girls would later dress up and dance to. Kishori was clueless as to what must be done.

Women in Cinema

In India, all those in the entertainment business have never been given any kind of normal reputation – they have always been considered less, as lower people who can be hired, whose labour can be bought. Of course, that kind of attitude has considerably changed today. In the 1930s or 40s, cinema actresses were not looked at with the kind of awe and respect they generate today.

Nobody thought of Shanta Apte, the great singer–actress of Hindi and Marathi cinema, as a celebrity, like Aishwarya Rai today, or someone you would like to meet and get an autograph from. On the contrary, in those times, people would try to hide any encounter or association with the actresses.

Change in the way people looked at artistes in cinema was gradual, and when it came to women, this shift was led by artistes like Durga Khote. Durga Khote was one of those few people who came from a regular educated middle-class background, and she made news for that. She shocked her peers by becoming an actress. If it wasn't for her, the transition would not have happened so easily in the initial stages. Durga came on her own terms and no one pointed any fingers at her. And things began to change from that point onwards for everyone else too. I think technology too has had a huge role to play in the way actresses are valued, even monetarily. Cinema and television have made them household figures, our role models.

Interestingly, when I was shooting for *Mandi*, I had taken Shabana to a *kotha* in Hyderabad – to introduce her to a madam from a *kotha*: her mannerisms, her way of speaking, and her body language, for playing the role. While we were there, a girl came and sang to us, wanting to impress Shabana, who was a star from Bombay; she sang all filmy songs. Bollywood music is everywhere, even the traditionalists are getting accustomed to filmy ways. I requested her to perform something traditional to *kothas* but she couldn't.

BLAZE
FILM ENTERPRISES
PVT. LTD. PRESENTS
A
Bhumika
EASTMANCOLOR
(THE ROLE)
Produced by : LALIT M. BIJLANI · FRENI M. VARIAVA
Starring :
SMITA PATIL · ANANT NAG
AMRISH PURI · NASEERUDDIN SHAH
SULABHA DESHPANDE
KULBHUSHAN KHARBANDA
BABY RUKHSANA · B.V. KARANTH
and AMOL PALEKAR
Direction :
SHYAM BENEGAL

Glossary

ada: gracefulness

alap: musical elaborations and improvisations without words, usually at the beginning of a classical recital

baithak: the lounge space

bhaands: traditional Muslim folk entertainers whose ancestors were employed in the court of Awadh

Chaiti: a light folk genre of music from Uttar Pradesh describing the moods of the month Chait (March–April)

chaturang: *chatur* means four and *ang* denotes parts. A *chaturang* is a composition with four parts, which may include *khyal*, *tarana*, *taal*, *tukra*, *sargam*, etc.

Dadra: a light classical style of singing, even lighter than the Thumri

dera/deras: groups of nomadic tribes from North India that went from city to city entertaining the populace. The leading courtesans of the troupe were called *deredars*.

Devadasis: community of singing and dancing women traditionally associated with temples in South India. Other names by which the Devadasi tradition was known: Patar, Pahadi Patar, Domni, Goegirni, Perni, Natini, Gandhari and Gandhavirni.

Dhamar: a Dhrupad sung in the Dadra *taal*.

Dhrupad: one of the oldest surviving forms of Hindustani classical music, which developed primarily as a form of worship

Emma Clave: famous French opera singer of the nineteenth century

gharana/gharanas: stylistic schools of North Indian classical music, these were identified with regions where the music originated: Gwalior Gharana, Lucknow Gharana, Banaras Gharana, Jaipur Gharana.

gharanedars: those who practise *gharana* singing (traditional musicians)

Ghazal: one of the most beautiful lyrical forms of Urdu poetry

Goekarins: a branch of the Devadasi tradition associated with temples in Goa

Jhoola: folk song of Uttar Pradesh, usually sung by women in the monsoon season

Kajri: derived from the Hindi word *kajra* or *kajal*, meaning kohl or black, Kajri is a genre of Hindustani classical music most popular in Uttar Pradesh

Khayal: an improvisatory genre of North Indian classical music where love becomes a predominant theme. Originally, the *khayal* was poetry composed in *raag*, and gradually it developed into a musical form wider in concept.

kotha/kothas: the permanent dwellings of courtesan families

kothewali: colloquial term for a courtesan

Lavani: originating from the word *lavanya*, which means beauty, Lavani is a traditional song-and-dance form of Marathi folk theatre. It is famous for the 9-yard saree which the female performers wear.

laya: tempo

Mandra Saptak: the lower octave

mehfil: traditionally, a *mehfil* is an intimate gathering for the purpose of listening to music; also called a *bazm*

mujra: a dance form evolved by the *tawaifs* with elements of Kathak, usually performed with Thumris or Ghazals

naad: the cosmic sound

nats and natnis (of Uttar Pradesh): a nomadic tribe that excels in dancing, and jugglery and acrobats

nautanki bais: folk theatre actresses

Nazrul: songs written and composed by Nazrul Kazi, a Bengali poet, who is now the national poet of Bangladesh.

raag: a musical mode, a collection of musical notes which are governed by rules about how they should be sung together; for instance: Jogiya, Adana, Malhar, Gauri, Des, Kafi, Kanada, Khambavati, Bhairavi.

Raja Harishchandra: the first Indian talkie film made by Dada Saheb Phalke in 1913

samanya: a woman who makes a living out of her beauty; someone who is available to all for a price or a *rupajiva*

shellac: important constituent required in the manufacture of disc records

shishya: a disciple

shringaar: adornments

swara: musical note in an octave. In Hindustani music there are seven basic *swaras*: *sa re ga ma pa dha ni*

Swarvarjit: a *swara* which is *varjit*, or not used in a particular *raag*

taan: improvisations of notes in medium and fast tempo

taar saptak: higher octave

taleem: the imparting of knowledge, particularly practical training, by an Ustad or Guru

Tappa: a form of Indian semi-classical music in which *bol* and *taan* are tightly knitted together

tawaif: colloquial Urdu term for a courtesan

Tarana: a popular form of Hindustani classical music which contains Persian and Arabic phenomes like *deem, tak, naa, tir, dani, derena*

Thumri: a genre of semi-classical North Indian music, which is usually romantic or devotional in nature. Thumri as an attitude of presentation is said to have *Purab* and *Punjab Angi. Purab Ang* is considered to be an authentic form of Thumri.

Vande Mataram: a poem written by Bankimchandra Chatterjee in the novel *Anandamath*. It went on to become the national song of India.

Wajid Ali Shah: the last Nawab of the Awadh region in the modern state of Uttar Pradesh in India. He was known for his significant contribution to North Indian music culture, dance forms like Kathak and the revival of theatrical arts.

King George V's visit to Allahabad: King George V's visit to the Imperial Durbar held to commemorate his coronation as Emperor of India in the year 1911.

References

- Amarnath, P. (1989). *Living Idioms in Hindustani Music: A Dictionary of Terms and Terminology.* Vikas Publishing House, New Delhi.
- Bharatan, R. (2010). *A Journey Down Memory Lane.* Hay House Publishers, New Delhi.
- Bhavita, B. (2015). "From Goa To Outer Space – An Interstellar Raga From India", 13 May. Available at http://www.untold.in/interstellar-raga-from-india (accessed on 4 January 2016).
- Biswas, P. (2015). "A Voice from Long Ago: Sashimukhi, not Gauhar Jaan, was the first Indian voice to be recorded", *Indian Express*, 4 August. Available at http://indianexpress.com/article/lifestyle/a-voice-from-long-ago-sashimukhi-not-gauhar-jaan-was-the-first-indian-voice-to-be-recorded (accessed on 4 January 2016).
- Chandvankar, S. (ed.). *The Record News Journal*, Society of Indian Record Collectors, Mumbai.
- Dasgupta, A. (ed.). (2007). "Embodied Voices: The Gramophone Company's Recording Tours, 1904–1907", in *Music and Modernity: Indian Music in an Age of Mechanical Reproduction.* Thema, Kolkata.
- Habib, I. (1986). "Non-Agricultural Production", in I. Habib and T. Raychaudhuri (eds.), *Cambridge Economic History of India, Vol. I*, Cambridge University Press, Cambridge.
- Hughes, S. (2010). 'Play it again Saraswati: the gramophone and religious practice in colonial south India', presented at the Women on Record – Think Through seminar, New Delhi, 29–30 March.
- Kalidas, S. (2009). *Begum Akhtar: Love's Own Voice.* Roli Books, New Delhi.
- Kidwai, S. (2004). 'The Singing Ladies Find A Voice', Seminar 540, New Delhi.
- Kinnear, M.S. (1994). *The Gramophone Company's First Indian Recordings (1899–1908)*, Popular Prakashan, New Delhi.
- Manuel, P. (1989). *Thumri in Historical and Stylistic Perspectives.* Motilal Banarsidass, New Delhi.
- Nevile, P. (1996). *Nautch Girls of India: Dancers, Singers, Playmates.* Ravi Kumar Publisher, New Delhi.
- Parthasarathi, V. (2010). 'Media and The Making of Selling: The Gramophone in Urban India', presented at the Women on Record – Think Through seminar, New Delhi, 29–30 March.
- Patke, R. "'Must Listen' list of North Indian Classical Vocal Music". Available at https://courses.nus.edu.sg/course/ellpatke/Miscellany/must%20listen%20list-index.htm (accessed on 4 January 2016).
- Pukhraj, M. (2003). *Song Sung True: A Memoir* (translated by Saleem Kidwai). Zubaan, New Delhi.
- Singh, G.N. (2002). *Mehfil.* Bihar Hindi Granth Academy, Patna.
- Strötbaum, H. *The Fred Gaisberg Diaries.* Available at http://www.recordingpioneers.com/docs/GAISBERG_DIARIES_1.pdf (accessed on 4 January 2016).
- Wade, B.C. (1997). *Khyal: Creativity within North India's Classical Music Tradition.* Munshiram Manoharlal, New Delhi.

KOHINOOR RECORD
HINDI DRAMA

Broadcast
BRITISH MAKE BY
PATENT PROCESS
B 2165-B
PREM JHULAVI JIVAROYA
Kafi Misra
Master Vasant Damodar
Marathi
HE MUSICAL PRODUCTS LIMITED

The TWIN
TWIN
HINDUSTANI SONG
F.T. 455
बड़ी लम्बी सफ़र को सैया गयो रे
MISS DULARI
BD. 2645
MANUFACTURED FOR THE TWIN RECORD CO., LTD., DUM DUM

HIS MASTER'S VOICE
Hindustani
Film: TANSEN
KHURSHID & SAIGAL
Ranjit Movietone
GRAMOPHONE CO., LTD., DUM DUM